W
A

uide

ood

First published in Great Britain in 2012 by
Need2Know
Remus House
Coltsfoot Drive
Peterborough
PE2 9BF
Telephone 01733 898103
Fax 01733 313524
www.need2knowbooks.co.uk

Contents

Introduction

There is nothing quite as exciting as writing a play. It is a journey through time, space and emotions, and it requires a particular energy from the writer to make it from the first to the last draft.

The first draft runs on rocket fuel, that initial energy of creating a world of movement on paper has to see you through all the subsequent drafts. No play is finished until it is performed and even then, your play is living on somewhere in your audience's head. Your play, precisely because it is a kind of map for performance, will live on, subject to new interpretation and always in flux.

But to write a play that moves its audience is a difficult task. This book sets out to guide you through the process. Whether you are a student or a new writer, this informative guide is full of the stuff you need to know and insight from a practising scriptwriter. Each chapter has activities for you to do and personal insight into the craft.

This book will help you to discover ways to generate source material, how to create characters with depth and motivation and help you to construct the skeletal structure of your play. It will lead you through three-act and five-act structures, help you spin a plot, guide you through rising and falling action, give voice to dialogue, advise on rewriting and where to go when your play is finally ready to go out into the world.

When you write a play, whether it is a ten-minute play, a one-act play lasting around 50 minutes or an evening's three-act entertainment, it needs to be like an egg, inside is a very good idea. When I write a play I can sense a good idea because of a sense of euphoria, it's almost like falling in love; I get butterflies in my stomach. It needs to be that strong to get you through, and surrounded by ideas as you might be, you will know that that idea is the one that has got *it*.

Use this book to discover and write your *it*.

Chapter One

Why Do You Want to Write a Play?

I am going to start this book by suggesting this is an important question to answer. You will have many days like those of Tenessee Williams, writing in his diary on 20th August, 1939:

'I write badly or not at all – Started a marvellously promising new play last week – but can't seem to get going on it – Dull, dull! I sit down and write and nothing happens'.

The good thing is that Tenessee Williams got over his writing doldrums and brought us such marvellous plays as *A Streetcar Named Desire*.

You will also have days with tears streaming down your face as you write a moving scene that you know is dynamite. You will have both because playwriting is an act of perseverance. It is a form of writing which demands humility and hard work. Even when an idea is groomed into its first recognisable shape, the work is not complete and draft after draft must follow as day follows night. The play is not even complete when the final draft is committed to paper and the playwright takes the script, nervously, to a group of actors for its first live reading. Even in rehearsal, there are rewrites, shifts and clarifications, small changes to give more intensity, flow or make clearer a character's motivation. To write a play begins as a solitary adventure but becomes a collaborative journey with directors, actors, designers, costumiers, make-up artists, composers, lighting technicians and promoters and, finally, the audience, who colour the words and performance with their personal insight, reaction and emotional response. But writing that play starts with you.

'To write a play begins as a solitary adventure but becomes a collaborative journey.'

I have made it sound a very arduous process but it is also the most dynamic, exciting writing experience it is possible to have. Writing a play is to live dangerously all at once.

Everyone needs a way to express themselves and make sense of the extraordinary, amazing and frustrating world around them. This could be your form, but there must have been something that has drawn you to it.

Make sure you know in your heart what it is. It could be that you are just attracted to the dynamism of theatre or to the romance of it. It is, after all, an ancient form with its roots running back to Ancient Greece. Maybe it is because it is also fleeting. It is there, in all its magic on stage and then a memory, a trace of emotion and image in your audience's collective head. It burns brightly like a candle and then the physical experience is gone. Maybe it is because the text is there in black and white, a map of words that will be renewed in new interpretations over and over again. Maybe it is because the audience is the final part of the intricate puzzle of the play in that they are part of the performance, breathing it in, responding, thinking and bringing it to life with their presence and every audience is different.

'Do not expect to earn a living from writing for the stage – at the very least not without getting a long way up the theatre career ladder or being a genius, very lucky, or both.'

I have often seen two consecutive performances of my own plays, same actors, same set, same performance; but both very different, because the reaction and the energy of the audience is completely new and it does impact on the final experience and how the actors respond.

It could be that you wish to write professionally for the stage and see your work performed. Do not expect to earn a living from writing for the stage – at the very least not without getting a long way up the theatre career ladder or being a genius, very lucky, or both. But do expect to make something, be excited and surprised and to work with surprising and interesting people.

It could be that you wish to explore your own potential and enjoy the surprise and pleasure of discovering what story worlds and characters you can bring to life. It is important to ask questions of yourself and of decisions about character and action, motivation and dialogue while you are writing. Questioning is an important tool to use in the writing process, as it is in life. Get into the habit of asking yourself why? Why am I introducing that character in that scene at that point now? Why is it raining when Dennis and Delilah arrive at the castle door? How does that feed into the action?

Read, view and wonder

Before beginning to develop your idea into a drama, it is important to read other plays, not just because reading plays can inform your own writing, helping you to develop a familiarity with form and structure, but also to keep up with new developments in writing. Scriptwriting is dynamic and changes direction with ease, like a weather vane on the roof of a high and very visible tower sensitive to the direction and power of the wind. Reading scripts will help to inform you how to write and what is being written about. It will help you to know what themes are being explored by other playwrights, how styles change, the subtleties of genre and cross-genre plays and the tone of stories being told. There is generally a shelf of plays in most bookshops and libraries. There are specialist booksellers and online databases such as doollee.com which lists over 100,000 plays, playwrights, play publishers and theatre companies, as well as stageplays.com. (There is a list of useful websites and publishers listed at the end of this book.)

Don't be limited to reading contemporary plays or plays written for the stage in Europe. Hunt out old classics and trace the course of dramatic writing from Euripides to Wole Soyinka. Don't neglect Shakespeare, but read and see all that you can. Soak up story and language, conflict, action and emotion, character, mystery and spectacle, and dissect the mechanics of how the play has been put together. Above all, wonder at what you read and see. It will help to inform your own writing. Euripides, who was writing 400 years before the birth of Christ, uses language which is as fresh and clear as anything written today and the emotional effect of his writing in *The Trojan Women*, for example, is powerful and naked. I will never forget reading this play in the early hours of the morning, cocooned by the silence of the night and with no distractions. It was impossible not to weep at the courage of the characters he created.

Read scripts at one sitting as if the story is unrolling before you on the stage of your mind. This is important because this is how the audience will see the play on stage and you need to be able to sense if the play balances time. Although the play is a text with a multiplicity of words, theatre is spectacle, and you need to be able to engage the visual imagination and see the play, its movements, silences and gestures as you read.

'Scriptwriting is dynamic and changes direction with ease, like a weather vane on the roof of a high and very visible tower sensitive to the direction and power of the wind.'

Read together

It can be a dry, two-dimensional experience to read a play in your head when it has been written to be performed. Read aloud to yourself or, better still, find some like-minded friends and form a group and read plays in a group for the pleasure of hearing multiple voices bring a play to life.

Read scripts but go and see plays as often as you can. There are often cheap tickets available. Go and see new writing at fringe venues and attend festivals. There are many. If you are fortunate enough to be able to spend time at the Edinburgh Fringe Festival, go to that too. To have that much dramatic frenzy in one place is an unforgettable and intoxicating experience.

When I was at university, my tutor encouraged us to write short reviews of every film, play or script that we saw or read. It was great advice. If you don't have enough time to write something down then it is worth writing that review in your head. Take time to savour the flavour of what you have experienced.

'Read scripts but go and see plays as often as you can.'

Think about a list of questions to ask of any play. The list could include the following:

- What is this play really about? What is the theme or premise?
- Who does this play belong to?
- How has the character been unfolded and developed?
- What is their emotional journey?
- Was the storyworld convincing?
- Were the motivations of the characters convincing?
- How does the play leave you feeling at the end?

Personal reviews don't have to be long, but thinking critically and analytically about any script you read or see will help to develop the same critical response to your own writing and you will inevitably develop an instinct about what you read and see.

Keeping up

Scriptwriting is part of an industry and it is important to understand and keep up with the industry of playwriting. Reading reviews of plays is one aspect of a complex web of information that will add to your knowledge and may even inspire your own creativity. It is helpful to do the following:

- Read newspaper articles of interest about the industry and the views of directors and established scriptwriters.

- Sign up for newsletters and e-letters from useful organisations such as The Script Factory or BBC Writers' Room. (See the help list.)

- Sign up for daily compendiums of news about the arts and theatre such as *Arts Journal Daily* or *Artshub*.

- Read the blogs and link up for newsletters from new writing theatres such as The Soho Theatre or the Royal Court in the UK.

- Sign up for news from theatre companies, especially those with an interest in producing new writing.

Reaching in via websites and newsletters will inform you but also give you a sense of belonging to a tribe of writers. Most of the sites suggested above are free. There are other scriptwriting organisations, which promote and support scriptwriters which ask for an annual fee. We will look at industry bodies and script reading agencies in a later chapter.

Now, you have plenty of reading to do – what about writing?

'Reading reviews of plays is one aspect of a complex web of information that will add to your knowledge and may even inspire your own creativity.'

The importance of notebooks

When I encourage children in their creative writing, the first session always includes the advice to get into the habit of keeping a notebook. I show them examples of 'right pocket books'. These are portable pages of possibility, a scrapbook of words, sketches, images, torn out stories, memories of taste.

Writers keep notebooks or work diaries. They are the store cupboards of ideas, strands of thought, collected moments, captured views, snatches of overheard conversations, a turn of phrase, everyday observations, a story leached from a picture or taken from a newspaper. They are full of possibilities, reflections and thoughts about the process of living and writing. They are beautiful, private tools.

Bertolt Brecht had a notebook with him right up until his death in 1956. They reveal his thoughts and spontaneity and the birth and life of his plays. Inside are plans and thoughts about multiple projects, ideas that go somewhere and others that never got made, or projects that spanned years. They are personal discussion boards.

The process of writing a play also includes the process of writing reflectively and critically about the work in hand. It can be full of questions, ideas, dialogue, title tryouts, random thoughts. It is the working slate-board, the living architectural plan of the edifice of words that will become a script and that in turn is the multidimensional map of the performance.

The Daily Pages

Writing freely every day before facing the crafted words of a play can be a very good imaginative warm-up, and since the more one writes the better one becomes, it is a good discipline to write what was described to me once as the Daily Pages. I cannot remember now who thought it up originally, but it is a wonderful way to start writing.

The Daily Pages is a freestyle walk with words. Think of a word or an image and just write non-stop for five or ten minutes before beginning to write your play. It is a limbering of language, thought and visual imagination. Whatever is written down may look like nonsense, but there is always something in there surprising and worth keeping, maybe working towards and developing into something. Sometimes if something is troubling me in a play that I am writing, I will write down a word associated with that difficult point and just write around it. It can help to release something unexpected.

Try it now. Take up a piece of paper and think of a word like 'stone', 'sky', 'deep', 'winnowing', 'wilderness', 'emptiness', 'joy'. Give yourself five minutes and just write down whatever comes into your head. Don't cross anything out, don't worry about spelling or grammar, just let the words slide out of your pen onto the paper . . .

Five minutes are up. Look over your work. Underline what particularly pleases you. Maybe all of it holds your attention. Maybe there is something there that can go on to become something else. Whatever it is it is a useful word-out. Date it and keep it and tomorrow do the same thing. Wherever possible give yourself time for the Daily Pages.

Finally

Before we leave chapter 1 think about your own motivation.

Plays are very personal and your play on which you will expend so much energy, effort and heartache no matter its subject matter or tone will be part of you. Why do you want to share this play?

Maybe the sharing involves a question, an exploration of a particular theme or situation. Rob Ritchie, a scriptwriter who taught at the University of East Anglia, says that all scriptwriters (maybe writers), spend their entire writing lives exploring the same theme, over and over again. It may be that the play is the beginning of a debate that needs to take place. Equally, it may be that the playwright wants to provide avenues of escape through comedy and laughter, and there is no deep mission. It may be that the scriptwriter wants to impart a sense of wonder and magic in children's theatre in a world where wonder and magic are disappearing, or find a way to explore the tensions and issues of being a teenager. You need to know why you want to write your play.

'Plays are very personal and your play on which you will expend so much energy, effort and heartache no matter its subject matter or tone will be part of you.'

Summing Up

- Be clear about why you want to write a play in your own mind.

- Read and see as many plays as you can to support your own development as a writer.

- Get into the habit of viewing scripts reflectively and critically, the plays of others and then your own writing.

- Keep a notebook/diary with you and write daily even if it is just ten minutes a day.

- Think about why you want to write this play.

Chapter Two

Inspiration

Let us start with Alan Ayckbourn who is, without question, an authority on inspiration. He has written 64 well-received plays, after all. This is what he said in an interview in the *Daily Telegraph* in 2002:

'Never start a play without an idea. This sounds obvious, but you'll be amazed at the number of would-be writers I've come across who try. They assume, I think, that if they start the journey, maybe an idea will occur on the way. Perhaps a map of where they're going will blow in through the car window. In my experience, this never happens. You set off and after several miles finish back where you started'.

Mining ideas and exercising imagination

I don't believe that ideas can be forced but I do believe that they can be encouraged. The first thing is to be open to everything going on around you: ideas, history, news, family, memories, your own and others. Develop a habit of taking an idea down an unaccustomed pathway. Remember being told off for daydreaming in school? I do. I used to enjoy my dream journeys, flying to imaginary countries, living in exotic gardens with quixotic robots, wandering into the back of a fairy tale. Dreaming is a good habit to have as a writer. Don't expect to imagine up a whole play, but maybe in that musing there is a starting point or a character or a character trait, a problem or a challenge that you can use. Overleaf are some suggestions and hints that will help to come up with an original idea.

'Dreaming is a good habit to have as a writer.'

Brainstorm

Brainstorm with yourself. Talk to yourself, as with the Daily Pages in chapter 1 which asks that you let yourself go with your word-mind and just travel with your thoughts freely. This exercise asks you to take an everyday object in an everyday situation and give it a twist. Here is an activity to try:

- Place a teapot in the centre of a table. It can be any kind of teapot and any kind of table. Visualise that teapot on the table. How many cups and saucers are there? Maybe there are tin mugs? Maybe there are delicate little cups with gold trim and a smudge of scarlet lipstick? Maybe they are grimy, mismatched, or this is a dead teapot full of decaying leaves and the cups are stuffed with soil. Your table is set.

- Now imagine the hand that is to lift the pot and pour the tea. What kind of arm and hand reaches out? Is it an old hand, a young hand, maybe it is not even human. Who is it who pours the tea?

- Next, imagine who is being served with tea. Think of as many questions as you can about this simple scenario.

a) Does the person being poured tea want to be there?

b) Are they strangers?

c) Why are they there?

d) How did they arrive?

e) When they leave, will they leave together or alone?

f) What hour of the day is it?

This is a very simple everyday situation but imagine if nothing will ever be the same again after that cup of tea. What is it that comes out of the spout?

Maybe this isn't tea as we know it? Maybe it is raspberry leaf tea because a pregnant woman is desperately trying to give birth before a certain date? Maybe the tea is poisoned? Maybe, that tea has miracle properties and restores hope to the hopeless.

Decide what happens when the pot is lifted and the tea is poured.

Write a list of all the possible outcomes you can think of for your teapot situation.

You are generating ideas from something utterly prosaic and any one of those ideas could be the starting point for a play. Take one of your outcomes and try to write an exchange between the two characters you have drawn.

Your family and other things

If there is one piece of advice all new writers receive it is 'write what you know'. When I think of this I think what is really being said is 'write confidently with authenticity'. Childhood memories and observations about families and people we get to know closely is an invaluable and eternal source for writers. But writing too closely, rather than taking aspects of someone's character, situation or tone can be limiting, unless what you are writing is intended to be autobiographical and then a whole new series of considerations come into play. However, the family can be idea-treasure.

Here is a childhood-memory dredging activity. Why not do it now.

Make a list of the following:

▨ Try to think yourself back to when you were a child. Imagine drawing yourself back down a tunnel of time.

▨ Fold a piece of paper in half lengthways, like a book. On one side write a list of the following: a season, a time, a smell, a place seen, a colour, a sound, a voice, a taste, something touched, something felt inside.

▨ Now write something remembered from childhood next to the list. For example:

A season – Winter, living in West Mersea when the sea was frozen and the shore was littered with giant slabs of ice. It was a bright, sky-white day. The whole family were together. Our dog jumped onto a piece of ice and started floating out to sea.

A time – 6am, getting up with my brother to do a paper round. The weight of his silence in the morning, the noisy way he ate. We didn't get on. If he spoke I would only argue whatever he said.

See what memories and ideas can be released that can grow into something new and unique.

The overheard

It is amazing what you can pick up on buses, trains, on the street, in shops and cafés. You will never be bored again. Listen and use.

News

News stories can be a source of inspiration, but remember other writers will be delving into the same papers. Scan headlines, read stories, local and national. They are triggers. Ask a friend or a writing partner to snip out a number of eye-catching headlines. Now select one and try to orally tell the story that might have been written beneath it.

'Stories of all kinds are a source of inspiration.'

Stories

Stories of all kinds are a source of inspiration. Fairy tales, folk tales and stories from history are all brilliant source material, if you extract a plot and make the story your own.

For example, my play, the *Potty Porridge Adventure* for children is about why Goldilocks was in the cottage of the three bears raiding the porridge bowls. It involves a Land of Always Breakfast, an incompetent porridge jester and a fussy Queen of Oats and a fairy oatmother, but the inspiration for the story comes from The Brothers Grimm.

When George Bernard Shaw wrote *Pygmalion*, he was inspired by the Greek legend of the same name, and Shakespeare used all manner of existing stories.

Pictures

Paintings tell stories. Pictures can be a great source of inspiration in a direct or an oblique way. It may be that the atmosphere of a Vermeer is what you want to capture in a script, all those open doors with light falling across domestic space could be reflected in the space that lives within scripts. It could be the detail in a portrait, a girl holding a dead bird, or a game of poker in the left-hand corner of an allegorical work of art on the vanities of the living.

Now you have the beginnings of an idea it is the time to look at the premise.

What is a premise?

The premise is the theme of your play. It is the deep subject that you are exploring and the reason for your play's existence. It is your play's final destination. It is helpful to try to sum up the theme of your play in a single sentence. Film scripts do this in a logline; a sentence or two which explores the underlying meaning of the entire work. It is helpful to write a logline for your own work. Play scripts benefit from the clear knowledge of what your play is about. A single sentence might sound easy but it can be the hardest sentence you will write.

For example, the logline of Christopher Hampton's play, *Les Liaisons Dangereuse*, an adaptation of the 1782 novel of the same name by Pierre Choderlos de Laclos, an exploration of human desire, malice and revenge, might be: 'In a war of seduction and revenge, love ultimately betrays all'. Shakespeare's *Romeo and Juliet* is all about the power of love even though it appears to be a love that is stopped by death. Is it? In *Macbeth*, Shakespeare is writing of the destructiveness of unbridled ambition. In Euripides' *The Trojan Women*, the theme is the true cost of war.

> The premise is the theme of your play. It is your play's final destination.

Activity

Think of plays you know and see if you can distil the theme of the play into a single sentence.

Can a play have more than one idea?

Yes, but your play needs to have one very strong idea. Your play can explore a number of issues but there needs to be one central idea. You do not want to dilute the power of a strong story.

Believe

Believe in your own premise. You have to believe in the truth of what you write. If you do not then nobody else will, and your writing will be unconvincing.

Summing Up

- Don't start to write your play without a good idea.
- Be open to ideas – they are everywhere.
- Develop the premise of your play.
- Believe in the truth of your premise. If you don't believe in it then neither will anyone else.

Chapter Three

Character and Characterization

This is at the heart of the whole business of making things up. Malcolm Bradbury said 'the power to create character is at the heart of all fictional writing'. It certainly is at the heart of a play. And the depth of the knowledge that you must have about your major characters is greater than you probably have of your brothers or sisters, or even yourself. You need to know your major characters inside out.

'Before I write down one word, I have to have the character in my mind through and through. I must penetrate into the last wrinkle of his soul', as Henrik Ibsen so beautifully puts it.

On the wall opposite my desk, there is a handwritten note. It says 'character is action'. I cannot recall where it came from now but it is a reminder of what is important to remember when writing a play. Everything that happens, every facial twitch, every line of dialogue, every action and interaction only happens through and in relation to and because of the characters that live in the play, and their motivations. But it also tells me that a character is an active force. My character is in movement, subject to change and will be going on an emotional journey. Plot needs character and character comes before plot.

Characterisation is the way in which the writer and the actor establish a character. This, at its best, is shown seamlessly through dialogue, action and gesture.

'Characterization at its best, is shown seamlessly through dialogue, action and gesture.'

Subtext

Subtext is the underlying motivations of the characters in the play. (We will return to this later in this chapter).

Dramatic character types

It is a human trait to dream of heroes, and no play can live without a central sympathetic character or an anti-hero. The hero, or the central character of a play, is called the protagonist and the oppositional character is the antagonist, of course these elements do not always have to be human but they have to be there.

'The hero, or the central character of a play, is called the protagonist and the oppositional character is the antagonist.'

Protagonist

In early Greek dramas, the protagonist was the leading or first actor, but in modern usage the protagonist is the central character or characters.

Often in Greek drama this character would be the title of the play, for example, Euripides' *Orestes* or *Medea*. Increasingly, it is the character with whom we have most empathy and who owns the story of the play. The titles of Shakespeare's plays often indicate the protagonist, for example: *Hamlet, Julius Caesar*, or *Henry V*. The protagonist doesn't always have to be heroic or a leader; he/she can also be an anti-hero, such as Othello. In *Romeo and Juliet*, there were two central characters, or protagonists, and equally, two indomitable antagonists in the feuding families, a character set-up which led to tragedy.

Another dual protagonist situation can be the coupling of two characters – who in some way oppose each other; beautifully carried off in the sad-funny 1965 Broadway hit, Neil Simon's, *The Odd Couple*.

The protagonist doesn't always have to be likeable, that figure can be despicable, but there must be something fascinating that is going to draw us in. The character has to be strongly enough drawn that we are going to desire to follow them on their dramatic journey.

There has to be something vital that the protagonist is at risk of losing if they fail to overcome the obstacles they face. The higher the stakes, the more intent the main character will be on fulfilling his motivation.

In *Hamlet*, what is at stake is his honour and peace of mind, his ability to be able to live with himself, now that he knows that his father was betrayed and murdered.

Antagonist

The antagonist is the major oppositional character to the hero or protagonist in the play, usually the villain of the piece. The antagonist has to be as strong match, even if not openly, to the strength of the central character. Iago is an antagonist in *Othello* but so is Othello himself, with his dark jealousy and morbidity. In some cases, the antagonist can be good when he is opposing a dark protagonist, for example in *Macbeth*, MacDuff is the antagonist and wants to frustrate Macbeth's ruthless ambitions but he is a heroic figure and his motivations are good. Sometimes, the antagonist can be more than one character, it can be the environment, it can be war, confusion or a system, it can be an emotion or the antagonism, the opposing force can lie in the soul of the protagonist themselves. Sometimes it can be a mixture of all and part of the above, but whatever it is, it has to be strong enough to oppose the protagonist and drive them to overcome any obstacle or fight to win what they most desire.

Mythic elements

Some characters, especially in the past, will embody mythic qualities and their stories will be large, historic and played out on a universal scale. There will be profound psychological roots to the way these characters are developed. These were often gods and queens, kings and giant rebels. Modern drama explores the dreams, desires and inner life and ambitions of ordinary people. The whole arena of character creation is in flux, as it should be, to open up new ways of representing human life. If this wasn't the case, we would not have had some of the great experimental theatre of contemporary times.

'There has to be something vital that the protagonist is at risk of losing if they fail to overcome the obstacles they face.'

At the same time, there still needs to be that central character that takes the audience on the journey of the play.

One of the early important questions to ask yourself when you begin to develop your script is this: Who does the story belong to? There may be more than one protagonist/main character, but I suggest it is vital to have an idea of who is going on the biggest emotional journey.

Minor characters

All characters need to avoid being ciphers but at the same time, you don't want to create a fascinating minor character who will draw the empathy and excitement from the central characters. These characters will often be static – in that they are unchanging, whereas major characters are dynamic and capable of change.

There are many stock characters which can be useful and are used all the time in film and TV. Personally, I think stereotypes should be avoided as much as possible even if they can be a base for creating comedy, and their stereotypical attributes can be magnified to make us laugh. I think all characters should own themselves, in that there should be something about them which is unique and only you would have written them this way.

Mining character

- Nothing beats people-watching. Observe and absorb how people behave in all different kinds of situations.

- Look at your family and friends and extract characteristics to create someone entirely new.

- Use stock characters as a pastry base but add in the new to give them an individual three-dimensional flavour.

- Real-life people – the story of someone famous or historical requires research – but it is your own interpretation of the character that is most important and will bring them to life.

▓ Aspects of the writer – in creating character, often aspects of ourselves slip in. Self-understanding is important in being able to create interesting characters and to extend them.

Creating character

'I like a lot of *Last of the Red Hot Lovers*. It is not modesty that makes me say "a lot of". I have never written a play that I thought was completely satisfying. The playwright has obligations to fulfil, such as exposition and character building that must be done. The trick is to do it skilfully. One is always so eager to get to the "meat", or the confrontations between the antagonist and protagonist, that one occasionally skimps on details. The mature playwright rarely skimps. I am in the process of maturing'.

Neil Simon (Los Angeles, Nov. 7th, 1977).

There can be no skimping on character creation. You have to know your character in an absolute way, probably better than you know yourself. It is no good just having an idea of the physical make-up of the character forming inside your head, or even his social status, you have to know his heart and what happened in the past that has formed him. Creating a character is like going on a long adventure of discovery. It is like being a parent, once loosed inside your play, your character can effortlessly surprise you, but to get to that point there are a number of things you must know, even if they are never mentioned in the script. The knowledge of your character's past, present and future will inform your writing. A good way to warm up your character-making imagination is to play with character creation. Try this now.

The pocket game

This game is best played with others because it helps to have someone trying to identify the person you are describing through the contents of their pocket.

If you play this on your own – write a list.

Think of someone fairly well known; this could be a figure from history, or a character from a book or a film. If you are playing with others then the figure should not be too obscure.

For example, who is this?

- A collection of wedding rings.
- A tutor's report on a boy's aptitude in Latin.
- A music manuscript, much scribbled on.
- A herbal preparation for gout.
- A sixteen-year-old's bridal veil.
- A handkerchief soaked in blood.
- A map of the kingdom.
- A petition for divorce.
- The testimony of a tortured man.
- Two orders for execution.
- A book of Prayer.
- A Cardinal's ring.

(Henry VIII)

Now, think of a figure yourself and try to put things in their pocket that describe and personify aspects of their life.

Next write a list of personality traits that are suggested by the contents of the pocket. Then take those personality traits and if the figure you created was male, put those traits into a female character, if female, male. Write a brief paragraph that describes this character entering a room. Decide how they would move, occupy the room, how they would take over the space, who else is in there, what they would say or do. Why are they in that room at that time?

'Character is shown through details and these are written into the script, but before these details can be present, you need to know your character inside out.'

The detail of character

Character is shown through details and these are written into the script, they can be seen as a series of instructions for performance but before these details can be present, you need to know your character inside out.

Write a list of biographical questions about your character. You need to know everything but start with the basics. This list of questions is based on a list I have cherished ever since it was given to me as a student handout.

- Age, ethnicity, gender and physical attributes including height and weight.

- How do they enter a room?

- Are they contained, ordered or bursting out of their clothes, do they brush their hair every hour or once a fortnight? Are they lucky enough to always look tidy no matter what, or can they never keep a hair in place?

- Do they suffer from illness or disease?

- What social class are they from?

- What social class do they aspire to join?

- What is their level of education? How well did they do in what?

- What work do they do? Is it well paid? Do they like working?

- What kind of working day? What is their attitude to those around them?

- Are they married, single, divorced, separated?

- Do they have children? Do they want children?

- What is their sexuality?

- What kind of home do they live in?

- Are they rich or poor?

- What kind of family do they have?

- What kind of family did they grow up in?

- Did their parents divorce? Were they an orphan, fostered, loved and cherished? Sent away? What were their parents like? Were their parents suffering from alcoholism? Depression?

- Were they neglected?

- What is their religion?

- Do they volunteer for a charity? Would they drop dead if such a suggestion was to be made? Are they well liked? Do people seek them out or shun them?

- Who is their best friend?

- Do they support a political party?

- What do they like doing? What newspaper do they read? Magazine? What is their favourite programme on TV? Music? Film?

- What is their ambition? What do they want? What do they think they want? What do they really want?

- What is their major disappointment? In life, in themselves?

- What is their attitude to life? Are they easygoing? Pessimistic? Mistrustful? Naïve?

- What makes them special? Abilities? Qualities?

- Do they have imagination? What kind? Do they trust imagination?

- Do they trust themselves?

Finally:

- What do they love?

- What do they hate?

- What do they fear?

- What do they dream about?

This seems exhaustive but it is an indication of how well you need to know your character. Even if the information you collate about your character is never revealed on stage, you need to know it. It will inform your writing and you need to do this for all your major characters.

The name game

What's in a name? Quite a lot!

Christening your characters is an important part of defining them. Names say a lot about class, nationality and age. A girl called Taylor is likely to have been born in the 1990s, whereas a Winifred would be in a gymslip in 1914. The name Martha sounds like the kind of name that could be given to a hard-working, dependable woman. Nicknames may be used and will reflect the relationship between characters. Sometimes surnames can have a significance embedded in them. Of course, you can use names that seem to signal one thing and then turn that meaning on its head.

In medieval morality plays characters were simple representations of one virtue or vice, such as lust, pride or envy, and were named accordingly.

Activity

Collect faces, postcards of people and places, and use them to inspire character creation or setting. Look through a magazine and cut out faces, or if you have postcards with people in them, pick a picture of a person. Try and create a character profile using the questions above. Before you know it you are bringing a three-dimensional character to life and starting to develop a dramatic story. Give them a name.

'What's in a name? Quite a lot!'

A character log

This is used in screenwriting, but I find it useful in creating any character for playwriting or story writing. It is a three-word description of someone – but it conveys the essence of the character.

Ask yourself to describe the character you have just profiled in three words – alighting on three characteristics? What are they going to be?

For example, my next-door neighbour is generous, obsessively neat and a gossip. She is neither good nor bad, but a mixture. In your character logs it is more interesting to have qualities that rub up against each other. Most of us have got good and bad traits, your characters need to reflect that reality. Your character is already looking dramatic if they have inner conflict before they set foot on your first page.

Inner conflict

The plot of the play will place your character in conflict with the world, but your character will need inner conflict between their obvious motivation and deep motivation; with the world and themselves.

Inner conflict works if your character is made up in such a way he has something to overcome within as a result of the person they are, something conflicting. For example, a highly ambitious individual crippled with self-loathing who self-sabotages their own achievements. A personality who has to be in control who longs to paint, travel and live among strangers.

External conflict

This is the kind of conflict your character faces when overcoming outside forces of opposition, for example, other major characters, probably the most common form of conflict explored in drama; and/or larger entities such as society, war, cultural oppression, bureaucracy or oppression. Your character can be in active or passive conflict with these forces.

It is better to have more than one conflict at work in your play. If you are writing about a strike in a cosmetics factory in a small town in the Midlands, your protagonist could be a young woman desperate to escape her working class background. She is forced to choose between a privileged relationship with the boss' son which could fulfil her dreams but at a price, the expectations of her community and her own conflicted sense of social justice and personal ambition.

Exploratory monologues

A monologue is a speech delivered by a single actor within a play. The best monologues tell a story and reveal character and motivation.

Before I start to write a play I will write a monologue for my central characters and just try to explore their voice. Invent a situation and place your nascent character in that situation and give them something to do like looking through a newspaper or building a barricade or thinking about a problem to start with, and then let them speak. It is a way to explore their outer and inner lives. In this text, your character can move backwards and forwards in time and memory.

For example, this is an extract of a dramatic monologue from Eugene O'Neill's play, *The Web.* (*Thirst and Other One-Act Plays.* Eugene O'Neill. Boston: Gorham Press, 1914.)

Martha: It's easy to say: "Why don't I beat it?" I can't. I never have enough coin to make a good break and git out of town. He takes it all away from me. And if I went to some other part of this burg he'd find me and kill me. Even if he didn't kill me he'd have me pinched and where'ud the kid be then? [grimly] Oh, he's got me where he wants me all right. He squares it with the cops so they don't hold me up for walkin' the streets. Yuh ought to be wise enough to know all of his kind stand in. But if he tipped them off to do it they'd pinch me before I'd gone a block. Then it'ud be the Island fur mine. [scornfully] D'yuh suppose they'd keep me any place if they knew what I was? And d'yuh suppose he wouldn't tell them or have someone else tell them? Yuh don't know the game I'm up against. [bitterly] I've tried that job thing. I've looked fur decent work and I've starved at it. A year after I first hit this town I quit and tried to be on the level. I got a job at housework – workin' twelve hours a day for twenty-five dollars a month. And I worked like a dog, too, and never left the house I was so scared of seein' someone who knew me. But what was the use? One night they have a guy to dinner who's seen me some place when I was on the town. He tells the lady – his duty he said it was – and she fires me right off the reel. I tried the same thing a lot of times. But there was always someone who'd drag me back. And then I quit tryin'. There didn't seem to be no use. They – all the good people – they got me where I am and they're goin' to keep me there. Reform? Take it from me it can't be done. They won't let yuh do it, and that's Gawd's truth'.

'A monologue is a speech delivered by a single actor within a play. The best monologues tell a story and reveal character and motivation.'

Think about what is revealed in the extract.

Another way to explore your character and to introduce character is to have another character talk about them. It can provide great insight of the central character of the play as well as of the character speaking. Get hold of a copy of *The Dresser,* by Ronald Harwood, first performed in 1980 at Manchester's Royal Exchange Theatre. See how he uses this device to reveal and build character.

Character growth

> 'Adversity precedes growth'.
> Rosemarie Rossetti, (American motivational speaker).

If there is one certainty in writing a play it is that your characters will be in motion, fluid, moving forward through a story and that within that story, there will be problems to overcome, things to understand, change to occur. Your character's growth is in relation to their reaction to the conflict that they meet.

Your character has to move from one point to a completely new point. They have to undergo an emotional journey and be different at the end of the play. In *Othello,* Shakespeare starts the play with love and ends with jealousy, murder and suicide. Arthur Miller's *Death of a Salesman* starts with delusion and ends with corrosive truth. Nora in Ibsen's *A Doll's House* grows throughout the play from submission to strength and liberation.

One thing leads to another and the first decision that your character makes will result in another decision on a long road to resolution. Character growth can be positive or negative, depending on the premise of the play.

My Boy Jack, by David Haig, tells the story of how Rudyard Kipling does everything in his power to get his son, despite his youth and physical unsuitability, into the army to fight in WWI. The play catalogues the rifts that grow in the family as Kipling's deeply conservative and passionate patriotism blind him to the truth of his son's suffering, death and the reality of the war and his responsibility for the tragedy that overtakes his family. The Kipling we meet at the beginning of the play, a determined, vigorous patriot who does not have room for doubt, by the end of the play, is a broken man in a world he doesn't recognise.

Your character needs to change and learn from everything that happens and what happens is connected to the inner motivation of your character.

The job of character subtext

Subtext is what lies underneath the surface of your play. It is the deep motivation of your characters; it is what they are not saying but what they really mean.

Subtext is expressed through dialogue, through ways of presenting information; for example, a character can profess to be talking about someone else, when the audience knows that they are really telling their own story. Subtext can be expressed through body language. For example, a man enters a room with a mother and a child. There is a pause and then the woman tells the man he is most welcome and smiles but she pulls the child to her side and moves towards the window. She is clearly signalling to the audience that she is afraid and the man poses a possible threat to her child and herself.

You may have a character in such passionate opposition to something, the audience suspects that there is something wrong and that they protest too much. For example, a character who rails violently against gay men may be hiding from the truth of their sexuality.

Activity

Think of a simple situation which is one thing on the surface but underneath something else is being revealed.

- A young couple are choosing furniture in a shop.

- A man is at the door of a house, he is offering to cut the grass.

- A schoolgirl is invited to a birthday party.

'Subtext is what lies underneath the surface of your play. It is the deep motivation of your characters; it is what they are not saying but what they really mean.'

Summing Up

- Don't skimp on designing and developing your character profile.

- Be clear about your characters' motivations.

- Know what is at stake for all your characters.

- Name them well.

- Never forget that 'character is action'.

- All characters have to grow in overcoming the conflict that they face.

Chapter Four

The World of the Play

A note about narrators

Playwriting is the most direct of writing forms, where the principle is to show what is happening rather than relay an account. The impact of the story is far greater if the audience sees it unfolding before them in a series of scenes. This is called silent narration. Noisy narration is a second-hand account of part of the story and so should be used carefully.

However, narrators can be helpful tools. They can have a detached voice, looking in at what is happening from outside and offer a new perspective.

They can do the following:

- Describe events outside the play that impact on it.

- They can mark the passage of time.

- They can vary the pace of a play. If a narrator comes in and comments on an emotional scene before another situation of rising tension, it can help to increase the emotional impact.

For example, in *Hamlet,* there is a whole section of the play which is narrated. It is the part where Hamlet discovers the plot to have him murdered by the King of England. He instead, has Rosencrantz and Guildernstern who were to deliver him to his death, killed in his place and returns to Denmark to wreak vengeance and face his own mortality.

This is a useful way to present absent action important for audience understanding of the plot.

'Narrators can be helpful tools. They can have a detached voice, looking in at what is happening from outside and offer a new perspective.'

Narrators who get involved

Narrators can also have a view about what is happening on stage and give their opinion of the action. In this way, they act like moderators. This can be a difficult act. If the narrator is prejudiced or judgemental about the characters on stage, it can influence how the audience react to the story. It is an ambiguous role because the detached overview is compromised by involvement and the narrator then becomes part of the action of the play. At the same time, a narrator with a viewpoint is becoming a character.

Narrators as characters

'The benefit of using a narrator/ character is that the emotional impact of the play may be heightened by the intimacy the audience has with the inner thoughts of this character.'

A narrator as a character is even more explicitly involved in the play.

The narrator/character is an all-powerful figure who can reveal inner thoughts directly to the audience. They can do the following:

- They can make comments on other characters without any return.
- They can freeze the action.
- They can move around in time.
- They can distort the words and actions of other characters.
- They can distort the action of the play.

The benefit of using a narrator/character is that the emotional impact of the play may be heightened by the intimacy the audience has with the inner thoughts of this character.

Another benefit is that the potential for conflict can be increased by the narrator's position – hidden conflict, i.e. heightening or headlining the subtext. For example, a character speaks very highly of another character but as a narrator underlines his loathing.

If narrators who act as characters have a truly integrated and dramatic role rather than just a structural device, they can be very powerful and more than one can be written into a play. This can give multiple points of view. These can be contrasting and conflicting views to the action.

Sometimes narrators can have a very particular place in the play. I used a singing narrator in a family play called *The Day The Dinosaurs Came Back*, my narrator was a character, a mysterious troubadour who would appear at different points of the play and sing a song, the song served two purposes, it warned the audience of what was to come, setting up an atmosphere of danger, and it also defused the situation at other times and punctuated the action of the play.

Narrators are often used in pantomimes to keep the plot moving and to link scenes.

Activity

Think of a quest or a goal that needs to be achieved. It could be that something is missing and has to be found. It doesn't have to be life and death. Create a protagonist and an antagonist and any other characters you feel you might need to put into your script. Write a couple of short scenes, now take your scenes and invent/put in a narrator.

How does the presence of a narrator change your script?

> 'Words are sacred . . . If you get the right ones in the right order you can nudge the world a little'.
> Tom Stoppard, playwright.

Setting

This is the world in which the characters and action of your play live. Your storyworld is your unique creation with its own internal logic. Whether your storyworld is the lounge in a beachside villa or a magical kingdom inside a mountain, it will have its own contours, atmosphere and tone. You need to know this world, much as you need to know your characters. In order to construct this setting use words, image and sound to give a flavour of what it is like before you start to write. I am indebted to my M.A. tutor, Val Taylor, for the following activity. I use it all the time. If I am working on a script, it occupies half a wall. It is a kind of mood board, a collection of pictures, photographs, words and sometimes sounds which conjure up the storyworld of my characters. I wouldn't dream of starting to write without it, and collect pictures as prompts, and useful images all the time.

This is a useful way to explore the storyworld of your script because you as the writer will be conveying the visual sense of the play, the spectacle, the tone and atmosphere of what is on stage.

Activity

Take a moment to sit quietly and remember an event from childhood. Write down what you remember of the time, the smells, sights, sounds and feelings of the occasion. Write a brief description of the world surrounding the event and how you felt within it.

Activity

On a large piece of paper, at least A3, create a storyworld using images, pictures and sounds, let the odd word and slogans infiltrate your work if they give it shape.

If you have an idea for a play in your head, use the world of the play. If not, try to think of a storyworld that might be connected to the following:

- A retired policeman who has escaped to a small, wild island.
- A ballet student who funds her studies working as a croupier.
- A deposed queen.
- An exiled tyrant.
- A stand-up comedian who can't face his lack of talent.
- An idealist who learns to love power.
- A woman who threw it all away.
- A businessman who can't stop making deals.
- A house haunted by secret tragedy.

Or any other character/world, you would like to explore.

Once you have created a sense of this world through pictures – see if you can visualise how that world might change if different events occur. For example, the retired policeman might find happiness and romance on the wild island and his loneliness will be staunched with love. How might his visual picture change as the story unfolds? Equally, whatever he is escaping, shame, guilt, criminal figures could find him, and wreck his carefully constructed solitary peace and bring darkness and retribution.

Before you begin to write your play, create your own storyworld wall or board and keep it going as you write your script, add to it over the process and refer to it if you get stuck. It will help to inform every word you write.

Summing Up

- Use narrators wisely.
- Narrators can be used to modulate the pace of a play, move it backwards and forwards in time and to freeze action.
- Narrator/characters can be used to moderate the actions and speech of other characters.
- Narrators can link scenes, create atmosphere and direct audience attention.
- Explore visually the world of your story.
- Keep within the logic of that world.

Chapter Five

Structure

'The human mind is a dramatic structure in itself and our society is absolutely saturated with drama'.
Edward Bond, English playwright.

Structure is the skeleton of your play, and onto this frame of rules, the rich creation of character and story takes place. It may come easy to some, there are natural structuralists out there in the world who are born as well as made. But getting dramatic structure right is one of the hardest challenges in writing a play. It is a good idea to take the time to look at some plays and to unpack how a well-constructed script works.

Read Shakespeare, Oscar Wilde, Terence Rattigan and Harold Pinter as well as Samuel Beckett, David Mamet, Caryl Churchill and Sarah Kane. Read anything and everything that is written as a script and try to outline to yourself the roadmap of their plots. If it helps, landscape the plots – and draw on the initiating moment when everything changes; what happens next? Are there cul-de-sacs, hills, troughs, and what is the final destination? Give the plot shape.

'Structure is the skeleton of your play, and onto this frame of rules, the rich creation of character and story takes place.'

Plot-thought

Plot is a sequence of events that happen to your characters. But plot should bring with it a whole series of unconscious questions that accompany the action so the experience of watching the play is involving. Why did the protagonist do that? Who is really responsible? Will he get caught? Questioning is part of the action and experience of the play.

There may not be a final answer and not everything is always neatly tied up at the end but even if there is no clear conclusion, no moral journey, there should be at the very least a large enough question to provoke thought. Your plots need to emerge from the interaction between your characters and events and leave your audience with plenty to think about.

Dramatic conflict

According to the Oxford English Dictionary, the Middle English origins of the word 'conflict' come from the Latin for 'struck together, fought'. In dramatic conflict there has to be that ancient sense of a fight, taking place, opposition and movement and ultimately resolution.

'Conflict is created when a character is prevented from getting something he or she wants. Action is the result of conflict.'

Conflict is created when a character is prevented from getting something he or she wants. Action is the result of conflict. Desiring or needing something means making choices and taking action. These can be conflicting desires and a play traces the resolution of a central conflict. The play ends with resolution of the conflict.

Activity

Take two characters and place them in a situation. Make something happen and decide what problem they need to overcome and the conflict which lies between them. Write a short scene. Try to include personality traits that will impact on the problem. For example, although one character is very ambitious, he is also obsessively private and must reveal personal information in order to get what he wants. What happens?

Beginning, middle and an end

Plays tell stories. It is just how they are told that makes playwriting such a challenge and the most exciting and dynamic art form. Aristotle in his book *Poetics*, outlined a dramatic structure based on three parts, effectively, a beginning, middle and an end; a resolution. Greek dramatists wrote one-act plays, the Romans developed a five-act structure for their theatre, and today we have a plethora of play forms. However, all of these forms share the commonality of a beginning, a middle and an end, and this applies whether you are writing a one-act play, a ten-minute taster, or a play in three, four or five acts that spans an evening.

Plays can move forward on a timeline that goes from beginning to end but there is also the freedom to flashback in time or to move forward.

For example, in *Kindertransport* by Diane Samuels, the play tells the story of how Evelyn copes with her guilt after rejecting her mother who put her on the Kindertransport from Nazi Germany in 1938. The play moves between the past and the present.

Three-part structure

- The set-up. This is where you show the protagonist in his world. In this part of the play you need to give an idea of the life the protagonist lives, hints of backstory, an idea of relationships and a sense of what they want, their underlying motivation.

- The 'inciting incident'. This puts the protagonist into a situation where something happens, a situation of conflict. Once this point has been reached there is no going back, from now on the protagonist has to go forward with the story. Everything is changed. This could be because of an external event over which the protagonist has no control or it may be wholly or partly because of a flaw/aspect of the protagonist's character, or both.

- The resolution. This is where there is an end to the conflict, or the situation finds a new equilibrium. This could be for a variety of reasons but somewhere it is because the protagonist is who they are. There is something in the character you have drawn which enables and is a part of the resolution, good or bad.

You need to write an ending that gives satisfaction even if it is an ending which has stirred up many questions, there needs to be a sense of closure at the end of your script or a question that is big enough to take away.

When children are being taught to write creatively in infant classes, they are often given a story hill, and on this they draw or plot their narrative in three steps. It is a very useful thing to do with the structure of a play – and although your dramatic arc will be more complex, a visual diagram of where you are going is always helpful. Doing this for all your scripts will help with a sense of the whole of your play.

Five-act structure

A three-act structure is the simplest form, and sometimes writing simply and strongly is the best form of writing. Another structure widely used, especially in Shakespeare, is the five-act structure. A 19th century German dramatist, Gustav Freytag, came up with the five-act structure. This analysis is known as Freytag's Analysis. He divided plays into five parts:

1. Exposition.

2. Rising action.

3. Climax.

4. Falling action.

5. Resolution.

Exposition

As in the three-part structure, this is the part of the play where the setting and background of your play are laid out. Information about the protagonist or antagonist is here. It is here that the inciting incident occurs which sets the story going.

The inciting incident in *Hamlet* is when he meets his father's ghost. In Ariel Dorfman's *Death and the Maiden*, it is when Paulina realises that the man who gave her husband a lift was her torturer in Chile.

Rising action

Rising action is what happens on the way to the climax. This could also be called 'cause and effect' because nothing in your script should come from nowhere. Everything grows out of what has gone before. This is the part of the play where things get more complicated, confused and tension rises.

Climax or turning point

The climax is considered the high point – the most exciting part – of the story. This is where all the rising action and conflict building up in the story finally reaches its peak. It is usually the moment of greatest danger or decision-making for the protagonist. The turning point can be considered the incident right before the climax, or can also be used as another name for climax. For example, in *Romeo and Juliet*, the climax occurs when Juliet stabs herself. Romeo's subsequent action is inevitable. This is usually the moment of greatest tension for the audience.

In *Death and the Maiden* it is when Paulina is left alone with Roberto (her torturer), she has the confession of his guilt, and we are left wondering if she is going to shoot him after all.

Falling action

The falling action deals with events which occur right after the climax. This is where all the complexities get smoothed out and we are on the road to resolution. This is where loose ends are tied up. For example, in *King Lear*, this is where Lear repents and is reconciled with Cordelia.

Resolution

On the whole this is the conclusion of the story. There is usually a release of dramatic tension, known as catharsis. There is a celebration of a new order, a new situation which takes over from the old. Mysteries are resolved, settlements are in place; the moral universe is revolving in the right direction. It is the ending, happy or otherwise.

As mentioned previously, sometimes stories have endings with a lot of unanswered questions. It is up to you how the story ends.

'The climax is considered the high point – the most exciting part – of the story.'

Activity

Take a short story that you know well and see if you can plot its route to resolution. If you make a diagram – write briefly a description of where the story starts, draw and label the main characters – pinpoint the inciting incident and the dramatic arc that the play follows right through until you reach a conclusion.

Stories at the centre of telling

There is some dispute on the actual number of basic stories that there are in the world, some think there is only one, the quest; others say there are 7 (a magical number), others 10, but there are only a handful of archetypal stories in the world and these get repeated over and over again. Knowledge of the basic story structure can help you to more closely understand the story you are trying to tell on stage.

In order to compromise, here are 8 basic story forms:

1.   Achilles – The fatal flaw which leads to the destruction of a strong, powerful individual. *Othello* is an example here.

2.   Candide – The innocent Jack of fairy tales – the hero who cannot be kept down. The optimist.

3.   Cinderella – Unrecognised virtue is recognised in the end. The dream comes true.

4.   Circe – The spider and the fly. The innocent and the tempter/temptress. For example, *Dangerous Liaisons*

5.   Faust – Selling one's soul to the Devil and the price that must be paid.

6.   Orpheus – The tragedy of loss, the loss of something personal and precious.

7.   Romeo and Juliet – Boy meets girl, boy loses girl, boy wins her back. Doesn't always have to end in tragedy. Love between two.

8.   Tristan and Isolde – The eternal triangle. *Dangerous Liaisons* is a good example again.

These stories can all be found in a variety of genres and forms and maybe in your stories there will be a mixture of more than one, a touch of Tristan or an element of Faust.

Beginnings and endings

> 'Everything has to come to an end, sometime'.
> L. Frank Baum, *The Marvelous Land of Oz.*

Where you decide to begin your play is infinitely easier to write than where and how you end it. If you have created a wonderful play, engaging characters, a profoundly emotional journey and the script ends badly, everything that has gone before will mean little. Your audience needs to go away feeling satisfied or they will feel cheated, by this I mean you will have fulfilled their expectations. I have read many scripts which have promised so much but in the end, delivered so little in terms of an ending.

As science fiction writer, Stanley Schmidt, once said: 'Don't mistake a good set-up for a satisfying conclusion – many beginning writers end their stories when the real story is just ready to begin'.

Disasters at the end of a play can be unexpected. I once watched a production of *Hamlet*. It was a deeply compelling staging and the play drew to its climax and resolution. It was at the very end and the stage was littered with corpses, Gertude began to die and uttered such a melodramatic cry in her death throes that the audience laughed. The ending was completely defused. That ending was ruined not by the scriptwriting but by a single moment of accidental overacting. What the audience took home with them was the memory of that cry and laughter and not the sense of tragic catharsis that should have been with them.

You need to know how you want your audience to feel at the end of your play.

Think about how you are going to get them to feel this way.

'Where you decide to begin your play is infinitely easier to write than where and how you end it.'

Don't close in a hurry

Don't end your play too quickly. It can be hard to hold yourself back, after all that writing and the end is in sight. But endings need to be experienced fully.

What makes a good ending?

- It needs to fulfil audience expectation.

- The best endings are surprising but foreshadowed.

- It is satisfying emotionally.

- It doesn't have to tie up every loose end or even provide an answer. It is fine to leave space for thinking or questions to be followed up by the audience. But this has to be your aim. It cannot end with questions simply because you don't know where you are going.

- The ending feels as if it has arrived naturally and in an unforced way, i.e. it is not tacked on.

- Sometimes a simple ending is the best.

Some writers know what the ending is going to be before they even start to write the play, others have the vaguest of ideas and others nothing at all in mind.

Do not worry if you are in the latter category. Everything in the early drafts of a play is mutable. As you write the first draft of your play, I think you will find that the ending will start to naturally suggest itself to you, and as you get closer to the ending, it will start to shape.

You may well find your ending just comes to you at any time. As you approach the end of your script it is going to haunt you and be with you 99% of your day. Make sure if the ending pops into your head you are in a position to note it down somewhere. It would be terrible to work it all out and then to forget important elements.

However, if you write with the end of the play in mind from the beginning and you never lose sight of what your characters want and if they are going to succeed or fail, the ending will be working itself out all the time. In my play *Lilies of the Valley*, the old lady, Peggy, loses everything and waits to die. To me, there was no other ending, it presented itself as I drew towards the end

50

and heartbreaking though it was, I knew it was the true ending. It also fed into the script so that at the end we are never quite sure if the love she longed for and found so late in life had ever been real or had been in her imagination. My ending tied up loose ends, we knew what had happened to Susan, George, (if he existed?) and Peggy, and so was a closed ending, but also we didn't know if George had been real or was something Peggy had made up and believed because she so longed to be loved in her life and couldn't bear to live with that absence any longer. The question marks an open ending.

Questions are good

It is always good to know what questions your play is raising, although your audience might come up with something you haven't thought about.

What are the questions? What is answered by the dramatic arc of the whole play? What is left open?

Characters pull the strings

Although it can be tempting to have an external event, a sudden act of God, a flood sweeping everyone away, an arrow that comes from nowhere and just happens to knock off the antagonist leaving the protagonist free to win the woman, child, golden horse, dancing bear or whatever; it is far better if the characters we have lived with throughout the play affect the events of the ending through their actions.

The ending of the play always has to focus on the main characters. It is better if any subplot can be tidied away before the main event. You don't want anything to detract from the emotional satisfaction or catharsis of the ending. The final resolution is a release from the tension of your play. Aristotle called it catharsis. For the writer, if all has gone well and the audience have felt something and got your play, let's call it bliss.

'The ending of the play always has to focus on the main characters.'

Activity

Take a well-known story, something short and complete, a fairy story will do if you make it your own, a story from the Bible or a science fiction tale. Think about the end of the tale – and see if you can see where you can invent a twist, write this ending.

Summing Up

- Structure is the skeleton of the play.

- Plot is a sequence of events that interact with your characters.

- Build dramatic action into your play.

- Follow a three-act, the dramatic arc, or five-act structure and ensure you have a clear route from the set-up and inciting incident, to rising action, a climax, falling action and resolution.

- Think about what your play takes from the 8 basic stories known to Man.

- Your ending needs to fulfil your audience's expectations

- Don't rush your ending. Enjoy it.

- Always focus on the main characters

- Decide if you have an open or closed ending.

Chapter Six

The Detail of Structure

> 'The art of the dramatist is very like the art of the architect. A plot has to be built up just as a house is built – story after story; and no edifice has any chance of standing unless it has a broad foundation and a solid frame'. Brander Matthews.

There is another note above my desk. It says simply 'make scenes do more'.

It is a reminder to me that a script needs to be full of layers. Many of these layers will be added and shaped in the process of redrafting, but it is good to remember that any section of scriptwriting can show us more than the surface appearance of story or be a step from here to there in terms of plot.

The first thing we need to do is to understand a little more about methods of informing our audience of our story and the balance that we need to create in the structuring of our play.

Exposition

Begins with the opening part of the play but continues throughout. You need to give your audience the information they are going to need to understand the story you want to tell as the story moves forward. This information helps your play to move forward but it is not a good idea to reveal the whole story all at once to get it out of the way. Only give what you need to know to move the action forward. Allow suggestion to play its part, audiences are very astute at picking up story. It is better to give this kind of information in a gentle, half-seen, effortless way throughout the play than in a clumsy chunk in the first scene.

'You need to give your audience the information they are going to need to understand the story you want to tell as the story moves forward.'

When this involves back story or what has gone before, this does not have to be delivered like a chanted mantra. Weave it in to the entire coil of words that will become your script. Yet beware of giving too little information which can lead to confusion – and particularly confusion over which character merits empathy. It is like walking a tightrope. Your balance has to be spot on.

Some plays have no exposition. They are the theatrical equivalent of the man with no name and will encourage a sense of mystery. If this is the case I think it is best to have in mind a very good reason for taking this approach that is part of the story you are telling.

Many old films used to get around the problem of filling in the back story by putting a paragraph of explanation in the opening credits. Voiceovers in film or narrators on stage are another possibility, but on stage this direct exposition may not be viable and more subtle ways will need to be used.

Exposition, telling the story of the past in the present, is best achieved by using the following methods:

- Make sure your dialogue is realistic for your characters in your storyworld. Don't write more than your characters would normally say – don't have one character say something to another character that you (and your audience) would expect them to know.

- Use subtext – let the audience pick up on the meaning behind the words and on half-revelations.

- Body language can tell its own story.

A good thing to remember with exposition – but it applies to your entire script – is *show, don't tell.*

For example, if I want the audience to know that one of my characters, Simon, is a serial liar and a fraud I would rather not do it by telling.

Cathy: You know Simon is a liar. He's always having affairs.

I would far rather show what he is and how the characters around him interact with him.

For example:

Cathy: Where have you been?

Simon: Oh, honey, I'm so sorry. The meeting overran and well, you know Jones, he's out, redundant, he was so upset. I had to let him talk.

Cathy: But didn't you tell them, you were coming to meet me? I've been waiting here for an hour.

Simon: Darling, you know how it is with these office types and well, Jones. It's not like he's going to ever work again. I mean he was really upset.

Cathy: Jones? I thought Jones was a woman.

Simon: Jones? No way, he's got the paunch and thinning hair of a man losing his teeth.

Cathy: I'm sure I met a Jones at your company once, and that Jones was 5 foot 8 with long, blonde hair nowhere near thinning.

Simon: No, baby, I should know. It's me who works there after all.

Cathy: This reminds me of something . . .

Simon: What?

Cathy: Last year.

Pause

Simon: I thought we'd agreed.

Cathy: What?

Simon: You're being unfair. I made you a promise. You can't drag all that stuff up every time I happen to be a few minutes late.

They look at each other. Simon picks up Cathy's case.

Cathy: Of course not. I'm just being silly. It takes a while that's all.

Simon: That's my girl.

Simon kisses her on the forehead

          Car's just round the corner.

Simon leads the way. Cathy follows. All the energy has gone out of her.

What is not said is often most telling.

Whatever you do don't tell a character something they should already know.

For example:

George: We have been fighting each other all our lives. Ever since we had our first fight in the playground at primary school in Willesdon Green, right through to gang fights at high school to our challenges on the race track. Now maybe it is time to lay down the gauntlet if our kids are going to marry.

It would be better to write something like:

George: Goes against the grain, this . . . but I'll do it for the family.

Henry: Me, too. My son is so set on your girl.

George: Thought of moving away after the last set-to with you . . . then they would never have met.

Henry: Suppose you would've liked that.

George: No, no, I don't mean that. What's gone is gone now.

George extends his hand. Henry hesitates then takes it – they shake then turn away.

Allow the audience to fill in the gaps.

Activity

Imagine a setting and write the following:

▪ Create a couple of characters and write an exchange where they are speaking of a shared history in a realistic way.

▪ Create a situation where one character is revealing information about a relationship with someone not present but known to both and at the same time revealing their relationship with the character in the scene.

Need2Know

Hurdles, twists and reversals

When you have established what your protagonist wants and what is frustrating that desire and following the inciting incident which has triggered the story in the present; there needs to be a series of obstacles to be overcome which increase the dramatic tension until the climax. These obstacles need to grow in difficulty as the play goes on. This is called rising tension. And within each scene there needs to be movement, often this is a status reversal. More of that later; first let's play a children's game and a game that is often played at parties. It might seem a playful indulgence but it illustrates a point about how the progress of ups and downs needs to play out in a script to make your stage story compelling.

Fortunately/Unfortunately is played in a circle but can be played by twos – and you can play this game alone if you just write down a list of possibilities of hope and misery.

The game goes like this: one person starts off a story and then the next person continues it by making up something fortunate that happens to the person, the next something unfortunate, (a reversal) – until the story finds a natural end. The subjects of these stories can be forced to overcome every disaster known to Man.

Try it now with these beginnings:

* Molly finds a winning lottery ticket on the road.

* A queen puts an end to the king.

* A young woman discovers she has a talent for snake-charming.

* An alien escapes from a secret military complex.

* The Yeti comes down from the mountain.

Or anything you can make up yourself and see where you finish.

The characters need to meet a series of obstacles that will frustrate their aims, and these obstacles need to raise the stakes as this will increase the dramatic tension in your play over time but good things need to happen too. It is just

> 'The characters need to meet a series of obstacles that will frustrate their aims, and these obstacles need to raise the stakes as this will increase the dramatic tension in your play over time but good things need to happen too.'

there must be an increasing intensity. This occurs naturally as if it is hardwired into us when we play Fortunately/Unfortunately and it needs to appear to be as naturally occurring in your script.

For a very simple example in a children's play – a rewrite of *Goldilocks and the Three Bears*, a porridge jester must find a way to make the most special, utterly perfect porridge or lose his head to a mean and selfish queen who has dreamt of the most amazing porridge and now wants nothing else but to eat it. (This is the inciting incident.) The jester has failed yet again to serve up anything decent. If he gets the chop, there will be no one to look after his old mother and feed his menagerie of animals. (This is what's at stake, not just his own head but his mother's too and his family of animals.) His first obstacle is his own incompetence; he cannot make porridge to save his life. Goldilocks offers to help him, she has an idea where the perfect porridge can be found which is when she goes off to the cottage of the three bears, but she cannot resist tasting the baby bear's porridge, the perfect porridge, and eats it all up. It doesn't look as if anything can save the porridge jester. But then Goldilocks has another idea and she asks the audience of children to help him by making lots of different kinds of special porridge. This goes some way to satisfying the queen but the porridge jester still has to get it right himself. But the children have inspired him and he finds the answer (imagination) and puts it in his pot. At last the queen is satisfied. His head is staying attached to his neck and his employment is secure. Until the queen has the next dream!

This was a play aimed at very young children. In an adult play the obstacles, reversals and twists will be far more involved.

It is infinitely more satisfying if the obstacles that must be overcome are linked in some ways to character flaw. In the *Potty Porridge Adventure*, the jester doesn't believe in himself, and doesn't realise that the answer lies in his own imagination. It is only when he starts to look inside himself that he finds the answer.

In *Dangerous Liaisons* by Christopher Hampton, there is a double-line of obstacles to be overcome, those that are part of the predatory, amatory chase and social conventions, overcoming virtuous resistance; and the obstacles that cannot be overcome, falling in love, jealousy and social ostracism.

Activity

Think of a storyworld and a situation – put your character into that situation, work out what is at stake for them. Think of an inciting incident which will lead them into a series of events. Now think of a series of obstacles that could frustrate the character's desire and have these obstacles increasing in difficulty until the final dramatic conflict.

Twists

This can be an unforeseen revelation or the introduction of a new character which shakes up our expectations of what is going to happen. It moves the play in a new direction and keeps your audience interested, but it should not be so surprising that the twist appears to have arrived from a planet in another universe. It needs to be a twist that comes out of the body of the script, it needs to have roots but still be unexpected. However, this doesn't mean that life is about to get easier for the protagonist, quite the opposite. Some twists are used in particular genres, such as thrillers, spy stories and horror. For example, at the end of a play about a haunted house, it looks as if the ghost has been dispelled and everyone can start to live in the light, but then the piano starts to play by itself and a door slams shut. The horror is back.

Activity

Make a list of plays and films with very effective twists. For example, in film, my favourite twist is in *The Sixth Sense*. I won't spoil it by telling all but anyone who has seen the film will know what I mean.

Write a scene where it looks as if a situation has been resolved and there is a surprising twist.

Reversals

A plot reversal is a complete turnabout within a scene and the progress of the play and is closely related to the twist. Reversals just go further. They are also related to close scene work – and status reversals. (see page 64). A plot reversal will cause the audience to question what has gone before and to settle into a new pattern of thought about where the play is going.

In strong reversals, the protagonist comes across in a certain way, following a certain desire and battling against the antagonist or his opposing forces, but in the end the roles are reversed and we realise that the protagonist is really the antagonist.

For example, Oedipus undergoes a complete reversal when he discovers the true identity of the man he killed on the road. It is information that is completely new to him and from happiness he descends into hell.

Crisis

In a script, this is the point where it looks as if the protagonist will fall. It is the moment of greatest tension in the play. Whether the protagonist overcomes this final test will depend on what kind of play you are writing. If it is a tragedy then it may be the final cut. The kind of crisis will also depend on what kind of play you are writing. If it is a drama about the relationship between a mother and a daughter, then it may be an emotional crisis. If it is a political thriller then it could be a revelation too far. It could be a psychological shock from which it looks almost impossible to recover.

Activity

Imagine you are a pilgrim on a sacred journey to a shrine which once entered will offer you the solution to a problem which will help not only you but your family. Your family have staked everything to send you on this journey.

Plot a series of twists and reversals on this journey building up to a moment of crisis.

Write this scene.

'A plot reversal will cause the audience to question what has gone before and to settle into a new pattern of thought about where the play is going.'

Need2Know

Climax or turning point

Everything that has gone before is part of the upward slope of a giant story hill. It adds to the rising tension. The climax or turning point is where everything comes together. But the pattern of the whole is also to be found in individual acts and scenes.

In terms of pace in the overall structure of your play, if this was a horse ride, the horse would have started out walking and moved up to a trot and then a canter, and then galloped to this point. This is the part of the play your audience has been waiting for, so now the pace can change. It can slow down so that every detail of the climax can be experienced.

It is at this point that character growth can be measured and acknowledged in the script, whether consciously or unconsciously. Whether or not the protagonist achieves what he set out to do, or resolves the situation is less important than the protagonist's personal realisation.

Inside every scene

Just as you need to see the play as a whole dramatic unit, so each individual scene is also a dramatic unit but on a smaller scale. This means that something has to happen in sequence with all the other scenes in your play. But scenes can do more than play out action, they can reveal subtext, character detail and development. They can be used to set up future challenges and obstacles leading to the final denouement.

▓ Each scene needs to exist for a clear reason and help to move the story forward. You must know what it is you want to reveal in each scene. The characters, their action in the scene and the flow of the action as part of the sequence of scenes. You should have an aim in each scene and make sure there is a link or transition between scenes.

▓ Your protagonist or a leading/main character should be involved somewhere in each scene because this will help to move the script forward.

▓ Each scene should take your protagonist step by step closer to their goal even if they are troubled, frustrated, broken and obstructed. Let their emotions show and colour the scene.

Ask yourself regularly the following questions:

- What is the purpose of this scene?
- Why do I need this scene?
- Does this scene reveal anything new about a character or the story?

Moving

Avoid what I like to call sofa theatre – two characters having a clever little chat while nothing happens. Wherever you have dialogue the characters should also be in movement. I don't mean aimlessly wandering around the stage either. Character interaction needs to lead somewhere.

Each scene needs to have a level of conflict however small.

Think about where you are going to start each scene, if you know what the purpose is of your scene, you will be able to start close to the reveal.

'Each scene needs to feel alive with a certain energy that can complement the emotional arc of the play.'

Pace and energy

Each scene needs pace, a certain rhythm. Each scene needs to feel alive with a certain energy that can complement the emotional arc of the play. Don't be afraid of writing in space and silence. Harold Pinter certainly wasn't. A good pause can ratchet up tension. The pace of the scene should fluctuate depending on its position in the overall dramatic arc of the play. The closer to the climax of the play, the quicker the pace should be.

Status reversal

A favourite improvisational tool in drama, status reversal, a master-servant relationship between two characters turned on its head. Status reversal is useful in close scene work within the dramatic arc within a scene.

What it means is a shifting of the power relationship between characters and it can go backwards and forwards, while first one and then another gets the upper hand.

In *Lilies of the Valley*, a play I wrote about the choices we make about love, Susan turns up at an old people's home with things for her mother, ready to prove what a good daughter she is (high status) but her mother has found other friends and is in no hurry to see her (status reversal). The two argue. Susan fights back by hurting her mother (gaining the upper hand – high status again), but loses that position of power when her mother puts her daughter straight and leaves (low status).

Susan and her mother have moved up and down around each other throughout the scene and for Susan, who arrived in a high status position, she leaves the end of the scene in a low status position, feeling humbled by what her mother has shown her. She needs to come to terms with the knowledge that she cannot take her mother for granted anymore, that she won't always be there for her. This is a shock and leads on to the next scene.

Scene endings

At the end of the scene, leave the main character with some sort of decision or imminent decision. Let your audience hunger to know what happens next. Line up a twist, reversal or a cliff-hanger.

Subplots

A subplot is subsidiary to the main story. It is a plot line that is complete and interesting in its own right and has its own resolution. A subplot should broaden the perspective on the main plot and enrich it. It can enhance an aspect of a protagonist's character, or theme, or amplify part of the plot. It can be used to move the main plot in a direction that it couldn't go otherwise.

Subplots are the focus of minor characters. It is their story. Often the subplot can fail although the main plot succeeds. It is a working out of another complication that complements the main story. It can explore any aspect for which there is no logical space in the larger story and it can be a comic aside in a tragedy or drama.

'At the end of the scene, leave the main character with some sort of decision or imminent decision. Let your audience hunger to know what happens next.'

Subplots can be anywhere in the script but ideally should end just before the main plot reaches its resolution or the same time. You don't want your subplot losing threads all over the main ending of your play; neither do you want your subplot stealing your main plot's glory.

Activity

Take a well-known story from King Arthur or The Bible, a Grimm's Tale and do the following:

- Describe how the story is put together: inciting incidents, turning points, climax and resolution.

- Then introduce a subplot. Work out what it could be, which characters could carry the subplot, where it would fit in the main plot, what themes it would treat and how it would conclude.

Imagery, metaphor and symbolism

Metaphor and imagery can be very powerful, enriching tools in dramatic writing. They can be used in the language that a character speaks or a presence within the story fuelling the atmosphere. The weather can be used to heighten tension. There can be a metaphor of a tree in blossom which can have special resonance for a character and represent something in their lives or something in their personality.

Symbolism can be a physical presence in your play through scenery, setting or props. It can also be written into the dialogue or action. There can be a symbolic act that is undertaken as part of the plot.

For example, in a play about a young lover who feels betrayed, a symbolic act could be the burning of love letters and this would be part of the action – or the return of the letters to the lover. In dialogue, this could be shown by the lover talking about how he can no longer bear to stand in the light of the moon or be in a place associated with his love.

Need2Know

Summing Up

- Make scenes do more.
- Let exposition slip out throughout the play.
- Show, don't tell.
- Make sure you have plenty of conflict – hurdles, twists and reversals.
- Keep pace – energy and motion in your writing.
- Create a subplot to enrich the main action.
- Imagery, metaphor and symbolism enrich the text of a play.

Chapter Seven

Dialogue

To write good dialogue you need to keep many distinct voices in your head and yet be succinct, say the most that can be said with the minimum number of words. You need to hear your characters' individual turn of phrase, the subtlety of their tone and respect their integrity and separateness.

> 'When I first started writing plays I couldn't write good dialogue because I didn't respect how black people talked. I thought that in order to make art out of their dialogue I had to change it, make it into something different. Once I learned to value and respect my characters, I could really hear them. I let them start talking'.
> August Wilson.

In this chapter, we will look at ways to let characters do the talking.

In the beginning – the word

The script you produce is made up of the words that you put into the mouths of your characters. This dialogue is completely interwoven with every other aspect of the play. It is the body tissue around the skeleton of structure and character.

Dialogue has to convey character, action and the premise of the play and has to be true to the character.

Playwright Lucinda Coxon puts it most succinctly: 'Dialogue is character, is plot. Above all, it is action.' It is through dialogue that the story moves forward.

'Dialogue has to convey character, action and the premise of the play and has to be true to the character.'

About writing what we say

Dialogue is, of course, also everyday speech. But in scripts it is not advisable to write dialogue in exactly the way we speak. When we speak, we get out what we need to say; but it might not be in the most ideal form and certainly not very interesting to listen to on stage.

For example, if we really transcribed every word in a real conversation we might find that there are a lot of filler words which don't take the dialogue anywhere but just slow the speech down and fog the content of what is being said:

- Hi.
- Yo.
- How you doing?
- Um . . . well, yeah . . . erm . . . you?
- Yeah, okay, cool, well, like, y'know what I mean . . . it's, yeah . . .
- See you bruv . . .
- Yeah, see you around.

We often speak half a sentence and shift course, speech can wander all over the place in response to changing thought patterns, body language and broken synapses. We revise what we are saying mid-sentence. If you know someone very well, then you will half-speak – make occluded references and have a kind of telepathic bridge into each other's conversation. Sometimes, we will see where a sentence is going and jump in before the end, finishing off someone else's thought process. (Very irritating.) We often speak across each other, talk simultaneously and switch off when someone else is speaking until we can break in. Our speech jostles up against other conversations, other sounds, background noise and interruptions, other flows of auditory information. Dialogue is played out on a battlefield of sound in life. It's not surprising that sometimes so much gets missed.

At the same time as we listen to what someone is saying we are taking on board a whole range of underlying information. Body language, tone and inclination, implication, foreshadowing, history and mood, class, social status, experience, desire, ambition, yearning, confidence, geographical location; the whole subtext of being human is sewn into the seams of actual speech.

Pretend for a moment you are Professor Higgins in George Bernard Shaw's 1912 play, *Pygmalion* and you will hear what I mean. Professor Henry Higgins was a phoneticist and was able to place an accent at 20 paces. He recorded the way people spoke in little notebooks and entered into a wager that he could transform the speech (and therefore behaviour and status) of a flower girl into that of a duchess.

Speech places us. It locks us into a position where other people's prejudices and preconceptions can play out. Change the way of speaking and you can dislodge the prejudice or introduce a new one.

We need to illustrate just how people speak in scripts but without an overload of tedium. Everything that happens naturally in speech and everything we learn naturally and read as a matter of course, we need to represent in dialogue in scripts with layers of exposition, character growth and development, rising tension and conflict in character and story – as well. Dialogue has an immensely powerful and pivotal role to play.

'Dialogue has an immensely powerful and pivotal role to play.'

Activity

Listening is too often one of the lost arts from a time when we could slow down and concentrate on one thing at a time and one person at a time, a courtesy sometimes lost in these digital days.

Take the time to go out and listen to people talking (be careful, you don't want to scare anyone into thinking they are being stalked!). It can be really enjoyable to lose yourself in someone else's conversation and you will start to wonder and fill in the gaps, creating a picture of their lives.

Note down – what information you can glean that tells you about their character, desires, ambition, history and hopes.

Listen to the different ways that people express themselves.

Build a portrait of a person based on a snatch of conversation.

The individuality of speech

How people speak is as individual as they are. How we express ourselves is the sum total of everything we have experienced and become. It needs to be the same for your characters. Their speech patterns need to reflect everything that has been and everything they are.

Character speech patterns

'All your characters need to speak with individual voices – so much so that if you covered over their names you would still be able to identify who is who from the dialogue alone.'

Each character needs an individual speech pattern. It can be great fun to work this out. There is nothing like playing with voice to feel omniscient!

One person may speak in a staccato fashion like an impatient machine gun, another will be slow and hesitant and use lots of filler words, never quite reaching the point. Another might have enviable and absolute fluency and yet another completely literal. A manipulator will use manipulative language, another may continually interrupt, another continually efface with a surfeit of meekness.

There will also be pet phrases, expressions and particular words that come up over and over again, shaping our speech footprint.

All your characters need to speak with individual voices – so much so that if you covered over their names you would still be able to identify who is who from the dialogue alone.

Listen to the people around you. It is a fascinating skill.

Activity

Take a selection of pictures of faces. Now to each one, ascribe a quick identity. Now put them in pairs – and invent a simple situation such as buying a train ticket or looking around a new house.

Write dialogue for each of your faces and see how you can make the manner of speaking individual. Avoid letting your own manner of speaking come through as default.

Speech and situation

How we speak can change radically depending on where we are speaking and who to. How many times have you heard someone who habitually speaks in very middle-class accents lose their aitches in the company of a crowd of working-class youth. There was a positive fashion for it in the 1980s when everybody in the media wanted the authenticity of a smart, working-class sound.

It is not just accent that changes, it is also phraseology, vocabulary, every element of our speech, how loud, how low, how often. We speak completely differently in a business meeting to how we would talk at a child's birthday party.

We have a range of ways of reacting to different situations in speech, and characters in plays need to be able to have a range too. Avoid over-simplification of how a character must sound.

Activity

Take one of your characters from the previous activity. Write some dialogue for this character at a variety of situations and change the delivery of dialogue to reflect the changed situation.

- Alone with your elderly mother.
- Networking with a bunch of media types.
- On a ship at sea with a group of refugees.
- At a very posh party in a country castle.
- With a lover.
- With a group of teenagers on a sheep farm.
- A children's birthday party with too many doting 40-year-old mothers.

Accents

There is an actress I know who will only take on a role if she can attach an accent to the character. If the role is neutral in terms of accent, she will ask if she can add a soft Devon burr or a touch of the Irish. Accents help her to feel safe; they help her to take a step away from herself and into the role. They are a masquerade. In a sense this is unhelpful because accents should never be a decorative flourish. In the cases I have seen, the addition of an accent has never detracted from the role but it might, so beware.

Accents are important. If you are writing a play about the miners' strike in the 1980s, set in Wales or Yorkshire, all your characters will need to speak with a Yorkshire accent. Accent will help to site your play in its home loam.

Another use of accent can, as discussed previously, be to disguise or be in response to others. A friend of mine would slip into a sort of general form of foreign accent somewhere between Russian and faux French in male company to try to come across as mysterious and exotic. It was almost unconscious on her part, and I have to say it worked, but as soon as the man had gone, her speech would return to normal. Accents can also slip under pressure. An accent and how it is used can be part of the way character is revealed.

Don't try to write the accent into the dialogue inside your script; simply write the need for accent at the head of the script.

Avoid mugging misery

Whatever you do, avoid the generalised way of presenting class-speak. I have seen scripts with working class characters all depicted with an inability to say anything with a 't' at the end or a 'h' at the beginning and sounding as if they are utterly without intelligence and all the same. This is also the fault of the director, but the writing itself gets lost in a shallow slurry of stereotypical speech that says more about the writer's prejudices than any revelation of character.

Period and place

Extract from *Alcestis* by Euripides:

Pheres: A bad reputation won't hurt me when I'm dead.

Admetus: I can't believe it, the utter shamelessness of old age!

Although these words were written hundreds of years ago, they sound as clear and direct as if they have been written for inclusion in a modern play. Historical drama doesn't always have to be written in a kind of thee and thou pastiche. It can take account of conventions in speech at the time without losing emotional intensity, integrity and simple, strong speech

For example, think of the way people of different status might be addressed in the 19th century and what degree of formality is used depending upon who would be speaking to whom.

Pace, rhythm and flow

Your dialogue needs to have energy and flow at different rates within a scene between characters and overall throughout the play. If all the responses are the same length it is like watching a game of table tennis and after a while your audience will get fed up. You need to vary the length of your sentence and responses or speeches, or your audience will sleep.

For example:

Jim: I would like to come in.

Jan: Well you can't.

Jim: I'll break the door down.

Jan: Just you try.

Jim: You think you can keep me out.

Jan: I know I can keep you out.

Jim: I'm the bogeyman.

Jan: Duh! Scary!

'Your dialogue needs to have energy and flow at different rates within a scene between characters and overall throughout the play.'

Jim: What is it with you?

Jan: I don't do Halloween.

Varying the length of responses within a scene has to marry up with the character and the way that they express themselves.

For example, this is an extract from *Lilies of the Valley*. Susan is very late.

Peggy: The tea's cold now. I don't know if I can get them to do us another pot. You know what they're like.

Susan: Mum.

Peggy: And I've eaten all the biscuits.

Susan: I'm here, aren't I?

Silence.

Susan: Honestly, you can't watch the clock like that. If I say I'm coming at a certain time, I mean around that time. I mean, be reasonable. I might've got held up in the traffic or something. As it was, my meeting finished a little later than expected.

Pause.

I'm sorry, okay. Come on, Mum, it's not like you're going anywhere.

Peggy: How do you know that? I might have a meeting myself.

Susan: At least, I'm here, okay. When was the last time you heard from Sally?

Peggy ignores her

Susan: Have you heard from her?

Peggy doesn't reply.

Susan: Thought not. Not since the funeral, huh. At least I bother to come and see you.

Pause.

Peggy: Your sister lives a long way away.

Susan: Get real, Mum . . . go on. She doesn't live a long way away from a
         telephone does she? Oh, and she can write, mastered the pen in
         those eleven, oh no, she made uni too, fourteen years of
         state-funded education.

Peggy: You two never did get on.

Susan: Too right. Smug cow.

It is better to vary the length of responses on the page. As this exchange goes
on, the pace picks up towards the end of the exchange after a series of
pauses. It is closed off by Susan's response and there is no more that is said
about Sally. But there is a visual pattern to the exchange which reflects the
characters and action. Susan erupts in with speech and impatience and the
delivery is fast, she brushes aside her mother's feelings and her mother's
responses and manipulation of silence slows things down until Susan gets
heated once again.

Activity

Write a short scene where one character is impatient and tries to move things
forward and the other is slower, blocking the pace of the dialogue.

The pace of dialogue will vary depending on the character action in the play.

You can start a scene slowly and the pace of the dialogue will increase as you
approach the climax of the scene. In a furious argument or a deeply emotional
scene where one character is breaking down, it helps to have spaces, and a
calmer variation of pace between strong emotion although we know the
emotion is going to continue.

This applies to scenes too, so after a furious scene where your audience is
exhausted, it helps to have a moment to relax.

As a general rule use less to say more, or use the minimum number of words
to say the most. The subtext will lurk in the unsaid.

Silence

What is not said is often as important and revealing as what passes our lips. Use silence.

It can convey great emotional weight and increase tension. Silence can give pattern and shape to your script. It is like light and dark and in the writing of it in, has a kind of physicality which will help to shape your script.

Pauses and hesitations can form part of the pattern of speaking of a character or form the shape of a scenario. It is not just the space within a speech delivered by a character but the silence and space written into the scene; the distance between something else happening. Sometimes the space is needed to savour what is going on.

And silence itself can have many different tones.

The silence in the space between an interrogator waiting for an answer from his victim is longer, darker and harder than the silent space between a man who has proposed to a woman, or the intense, private, painful silence of a parent grieving.

Don't forget that your dialogue is supposed to make your audience feel something.

Tone

Tone is the attitude of the writer to the play being written. The tone of a play can be light, tragic, serious, ironic or whimsical. Tone is present in dialogue and in a symbiotic relationship with the overall mood or atmosphere of the play. The play will have an overall tone but it needs to vary within scenes.

If the tone doesn't vary enough the play will be dull and so will the dialogue.

In *Hamlet*, the overall tone is dark but it is also ironic, melancholy, passionate, contemplative, desperate and violent.

Phone conversations in scripts

Using the telephone in a script can be fraught with bad writing. You need to present one side of the conversation in such a way your audience understands the responses on the other end of the phone, without repeating them.

What needs to happen is an understanding of the gist of the conversation and a sense of the tension.

For example:

This is a phone call from *Lilies of the Valley*. We already know that Sally is Susan's sister and she is speaking to her on the phone.

Susan: I think you should get in touch with her. Why should it always be me?

Beat.

Yeah, she's doing alright considering. Personally, I thought it would take her longer to get over it – the funeral and all that. She still talks about him.

She wants me to get her a kettle and stuff – you wouldn't believe the time she called. 7.30. Can you believe it?

No! 7.30 in the morning. I swear she's going senile. Yeah, and that is another thing, buying her kettles and stuff, all that costs money.

I do talk to her about the house, of course I do. Yes. Well, why don't you? You're leaving it all to me and it isn't fair. How should I know? I don't think we should get her to sell it right now, not in the present climate . . . I think we should rent it out. She won't listen to me. That's why I think you should talk to her about it.

Beat.

Because you were always her favourite!

I've taken up tennis. What Vlado doesn't know about after-match massage . . .

No, why should Jeremy have anything to do with how I choose to spend my time?

I knew it was a mistake telling you.

Let me know about Christmas. You can play at being aunty.

Susan hasn't repeated anything that Sally has said – but we get the gist of what is being said, learn something about the relationship between the two of them and learn about Susan, her life, relationships, the theme of the play and move the action forward.

Activity

Think of a character who needs to make a telephone call. Who are they calling? Write the script for that call.

A multitude of voices on stage at once

'If your character is silent on stage, make sure that the silence is part of the action of the scene.'

Budget restrictions mean that many modern plays never have more than 2 or 3 roles but in the wonderful situation where you have unlimited funds and a cast of many, it is necessary to think carefully about the choreography involved with multiple characters on stage.

Avoid giving a character a remark just because they are on stage but have nothing to do. If they have no purpose in the scene, they really shouldn't be there. If your character is silent on stage, make sure that the silence is part of the action of the scene. You must know what is going on in their heads and the purpose of their silence and how it feeds into the rest of the action on stage.

Activity

Imagine writing a scene at a party. What conversations are you going to select to show to the audience? How are you going to write this scene?

Have a go.

Dialogue and its underside

Every character in your play will have a reason for everything they say. You need to know that reason. Your characters will take off with their own voices and you may write a draft and see the subtext emerging, character revelation and their true desires. You will probably end up with far too much.

In subsequent rewrites pare it back. Less is usually more.

Activity

Write a short scene where your characters reveal something about themselves through an everyday conversation.

Poetic or stylized dialogue

Not all plays are naturalistic. You may wish to write in a form that is very theatrical, very removed from reality that clearly states the presence of the author in every syllable. The script is self-consciously theatrical and aware.

When Shakespeare was alive theatre was poetic, but these days most theatre is written in a naturalist form. There are exceptions; verse plays like *Under Milk Wood* by Dylan Thomas or T.S. Eliot's *Murder in the Cathedral*. Creating poetic, powerful language for its own sake may be very tempting but not everybody can get away with it and audiences may not be as open to this form of theatre from a new writer. At the same time, if this is how you want to write, find a way. Just make sure that your poetic dialogue still does the job of naturalist dialogue, reveals character and moves the plot along. It is not enough for your words to be enchanting. They have to work in service to the story.

Epic or Brechtian theatre also uses dialogue in a non-naturalistic way, in that the characters stop to address the audience directly about the action taking place on stage. It is a self-conscious and artificial device. Symbolist, expressionist and surreal theatre all play with non-naturalist forms of expression.

Absurdist theatre is a form of writing where dialogue can wander away from naturalism. Although, in a play like Samuel Beckett's *Waiting for Godot*, the language appears unadorned, no one has a clear grasp of the language they are using and there is an obvious artificiality.

Activity

Read Dylan Thomas' *Under Milk Wood* and see how poetic language meets dramatic need.

What is the writer's voice?

A lot is written about the writer's voice. It is the individual and invisible hallmark on a piece of writing that marks it out as belonging to a particular writer. It makes Pinter 'Pinteresque' and Tom Stoppard 'Stoppardian' – an intellectual minuet around the puzzles of morality. It is a matter of style, about how a work is written but it is also to do with the choice of theme that you as a writer will explore over and over again.

You may not be aware of what it is yet but you will and you will then be able to explore different aspects of that theme. This theme is likely to come up in whatever you are writing even if it has a completely different subject matter, therefore, if you are exploring mother and daughter relationships, that archetypal relationship will emerge somewhere if there is the smallest opportunity without any effort in any script that you are writing.

The story you write will be unique to you based on the kind of person you are, your viewpoint on the world and your own personal life experience.

Summing Up

- Dialogue has to convey, character, action, premise and tone.

- Don't write dialogue the way people actually talk. You need to trim it.

- If you don't have to say it, then don't. Let your audience surmise.

- Use silence but always know why it is there.

- All dialogue needs pace, rhythm and flow.

- Vary tone.

- Make your audience feel. Dialogue needs to convey emotion.

Chapter Eight

Script Format and Rewriting

Script format

It is worth making sure that your script is professionally presented. There is no single way to lay out a play script although there are very strict conventions in place for film, television and radio. For plays, there is a general convention but the most important thing to remember is to be clear and organised in your presentation so that your script is easily understandable on first sight.

It is advisable to do the following:

- Make sure your script is typewritten.

- Leave plenty of space – wide margins top and bottom so that it is easy to see the script on the page – and to mark up/make notes, not very green, but necessary.

- Use A4 paper.

- Use 12 pt Arial or Courier New (both easy to read).

- On the cover page write the title, your name, contact details and a date.

- Don't forget to number your pages.

- Don't forget to staple or clip the pages together.

- Provide a list of characters with brief descriptions.

- For the scripted pages, the general convention is that the name of the character is on the left of the page – with the dialogue indented.

'It is worth making sure that your script is professionally presented.'

- The scene setting and stage directions should be presented in italics or underlined. Stage directions within a speech should be placed inside brackets.

- Double space between characters and stage directions but single line spacing within the script.

- Don't forget to put copyright on the title page. To do this insert the © symbol, write your name and date.

Example

Scene 1:

It is 1905 on a shabby Edwardian street. A woman about 40 stands under a gas light. She is plain and neat, someone's maid. She holds a small bag like a shield.

Robert Redfield, in his seventies, stumbles to his door. He has been drinking. He speaks without turning.

Redfield: You again.

     Beat

     What do you want of me?

     The woman faces him square on.

Redfield: I don't know how long you think you are going to keep this up but if you are trying to intimidate me it's not working.

     Redfield approaches her.

     People are talking. Is that what you want? Is that why you come here day after day? You want to ruin my reputation. You know what they are saying, not to my face, no, never to my face but I know what they mutter behind their fingers.

(softly)   I might be half-blind these days but not you. I'd remember.

     Redfield flails at the air.

     You women are like weights.

     Well, Madam . . . you are not hanging around my neck. Do you hear?

The most important thing to remember is that your script needs to be easy to read and to be clear.

Film, television and radio scripts follow slightly different conventions and these are important to follow because the page layout is related to screen time. If you are writing a film/television or radio script there is some useful software available.

- Scriptsmart Plus and Gold can be downloaded free from the Writer's Room on the BBC website. http://www.bbc.co.uk/writersroom/scriptsmart/index.shtml
- Final Draft screenwriting software can be bought and downloaded from the Web.

Rewriting

This is where you will really shape your writing and where you will require the greatest amount of stamina and determination.

You have just written your first draft and you have a great sense of satisfaction and achievement. You can definitely go away and have that glass of wine, pint of cider or cup of hot chocolate or do something that will make you happy. You deserve to reward yourself. It is quite an achievement to get as far as you have with such a challenging writing form.

Pause and take a break.

But this first draft is only the beginning of many more drafts. It might seem daunting; the idea of taking your script and subjecting it to more scrutiny and more drafts but this is the only way to come up with a performance-ready play. You owe it to yourself as a writer and to the play which you have brought into existence to give it all you've got.

Read your draft out loud one final time to yourself and put it away in a drawer.

You need to give your first draft, as far as possible, some space. You need to sleep on it or if possible leave it for at least 3 weeks if you can. You might not have the luxury of so much time but you do need to have some distance between what you have written and what you are going to write to improve, reshape or enrich in your second and subsequent drafts.

'Writing is re-writing.'
Paul Abbott

How many drafts?

It is difficult to say. Some plays will take a second draft but another will still be being revised 8 to 10 drafts later. Most screenplays will have a minimum of 10 and up to 20 redrafts. You will have a sense of when your play is complete enough to send out to theatre companies for production or to enter a competition.

While you are leaving your work to lie fallow, this doesn't mean that you will enter a state of amnesia over your work and your story. It gives you time to think and to allow things to come to you about your play. Note them down in your notebook. Make a list of things you think might improve your play. Little things that you know will reveal more about a character, action that needs to turn. These are little changes, a kind of polishing, but there might be larger structural changes that you need to deliver. For example, I had a play which needed an entirely new character – a requirement of the commissioning agent. This was a huge change and the rewrite was like writing the play all over again. Sometimes you will have to be bold and alter the entire direction or the emphasis of your play. You might even think that you have to experiment with tone and style. Don't be afraid to make big changes in your drafts. The thing to remember is that it is a draft, and your goal is to rewrite your play until it is as good as it can be.

'When you are rewriting it is good to remind yourself of the motivations of your characters, map out your turning points, twists and climaxes.'

Don't hack or wreck! Don't lay into your prose with a hammer or chop back the dialogue to such an extent it loses flow. You just need to look at what you are writing with fresh eyes and you will see the flaws.

Number all your drafts and save them all individually so if something doesn't work out you can always go back to an earlier draft and work forwards from there.

When you are rewriting it is good to remind yourself of the motivations of your characters, map out your turning points, twists and climaxes. Look at each scene closely and check that scene is doing all the work it can, that it is showing and not telling. Is your play well constructed? Is your play moving enough? Are you saying what you want to clearly enough?

Ask yourself questions all the time. Finally, does it have its own impetus, an energy running through it that makes it an enlivening and exciting and deeply emotional experience? Is that what you want? How do you feel at the end?

Finally, in this process why not get a group of local actors/friends together and have them read your play. You should not participate because you need to make notes. It is one thing to read on paper with all the character voices in your head and quite another to hear your words interpreted and sung out. It is an immensely useful process and you will find it helps you to see where cuts or clarifications need to be made.

Actors can have great insight into scripts and they will give you feedback if you ask. It is a real bonus and nearly always worth hearing.

The big thing

Do not feel disheartened or that you can't really do it and give up. This is the time for you to dig up all your determination. It is the hardest kind of writing precisely because you use the minimum number of words to show the most in-depth, multilayered experience in a structured way.

Enjoy the process

Rewriting can be the most enjoyable part of your writing experience. After all, you have got the story down and now what you need to do is just to make it shine!

Trust your instincts.

Remember only you can write your play the way you do whether anyone likes it or not. You are the writer and you are in control of your ideas, words and the creation that you have crafted. Enjoy that control. Flex your writing fingers and enjoy the process.

Summing Up

- Ensure you present your script professionally.
- Your script needs to be easy to read.
- Give your play some space – leave it in a drawer for a while.
- Keep focused and determined.
- Number your drafts and don't be afraid to make big changes .
- Shine up every word.
- Trust your instincts.

Chapter Nine

What to Do With Your Finished Play

Sending it out

Unlike novels and poetry, where you can send your work to an agent or a publisher, getting your work out there as a playwright is difficult. This is because a play is written to be performed. It is not just a private pleasure on the page. There are a few things you can do. Personally, where possible, I would do all three options listed below and take any opportunity to get your work out:

* You can submit your play to new writing competitions.

* You can send your play out unsolicited to theatre companies.

* You can stage your play yourself.

Remember

* Wherever you submit your play make sure it is presented professionally.

* Send a clean, word-processed copy (never send your original).

* Make sure the pages are numbered and fastened.

* Keep it simple. Do not send anything except the script and a covering letter. No explanations, no background notes or briefings. The only thing of interest is your script.

* Keep your covering letter brief. Mention only what is relevant. Be modest.

'Getting your work out there as a playwright is difficult. This is because a play is written to be performed. It is not just a private pleasure on the page.'

Don't say things like 'This is the best play I have ever written and you are going to love it!' Include a brief CV about your scriptwriting if you feel it is relevant.

- Make sure that you have done some research and you are sending your script to a named individual. It is not hard, visit the website of the theatre company or make a phone call and ask. It is a matter of respect, thoroughness and knowledge of the company, 'Dear Sir/Madam' will show a lack of all three of the above.

- In your covering letter include a short paragraph which describes your play, its main characters and theme. This is worth spending time on. Get it right but keep it brief. I am talking 50 words here. In screenwriting this would be a simple logline.

- Make sure you put the correct postage on. You will not gain in popularity and your script may be refused if the postage is not paid.

- Include an SAE if you want acknowledgement that your script has arrived.

- You can include return postage and an SAE or you can allow your script to be recycled. It may not be worth your while to have it back since you will want to send out clean scripts to your prospective script readers.

- Some theatre companies and competitions will take email submissions but you should always check first. Send your play as an attachment – a PDF file is best then the format will remain intact as it makes its digital journey.

- Always go for brief, direct and business-like approaches in all your correspondence and dealings with any theatre company or competition organiser.

New writing competitions

There are many new writing opportunities. Often they take the form of inviting submissions for one-page scripts or ten-minute plays or one-act plays. It is worth entering these. Often, all they can offer is a script-in-hand reading but it is a worthy way of getting your work performed and noticed.

Look out for these opportunities. They can be advertised locally and nationally. Sign up for Art News which is a free email newsletter provided by The Arts Council. (There is a list of useful website addresses at the end).

Calls for submissions are often made here. Sign up for local arts forum newsletters too.

Sign up for The BBC Writer's Room newsletter which will detail playwriting opportunities. http://www.bbc.co.uk/writersroom/

New writing theatres and small touring companies

In every region in the UK there are theatres on the lookout for new writing. It is worth finding out where they are and submitting your work to them. Some of these theatres will offer script reading services. Often they will have an annual festival of new writing but these can be highly competitive and their new writers will often have new work on but already be fairly well-known playwrights.

The British Theatre Guide lists theatre companies with an interest in new writing. It is a list that can change because many companies will be small touring companies that come and go. http://www.britishtheatreguide.info

If you send your work to a theatre company make sure it is one which puts on plays like yours. There is no point sending a children's play to a theatre that only ever produces adult theatre. If it is a touring company that only ever puts on Alan Bennett and Alan Ayckbourn, it's not likely to be interested in your two-woman historical drama about the Black Death.

After you have sent your work to a theatre company, do not expect a quick response. It can take anything up to six months. The company may not give you any in-depth analysis of your work when it is returned to you unless they have an interest in you and your work. Even if you are offered a meeting, this doesn't mean they will produce your work. They may be interested to see what other ideas you have or just to start developing a relationship. It means they see you have promise.

'If you send your work to a theatre company make sure it is one which puts on plays like yours.'

Staging your play yourself

This is another option. There are two levels.

A lot of theatre goes on in non-theatrical venues these days, in pubs and clubs. Pubs are definitely a more economical option than hiring a studio theatre. There are some small companies who perform regularly in particular pub venues. You could approach the company with your script, bearing in mind that there may be compromises to be made in staging. If the company is very small there may only be 2-3 actors, very little available in terms of backdrop or costume and props, and no lighting to speak of. You will have to be flexible and resourceful to begin to do your work justice. However, venues like this with the right company can result in great performances and invaluable experience.

Intimate spaces favour particular kinds of plays. If you are going to put on your play think of the venue that will best suit your story. An intimate, small scale play would be swamped on the big, main stage of a large theatre.

'Intimate spaces favour particular kinds of plays.'

Written, directed and produced

You can decide to do the whole thing yourself. In this case you have the option of directing your own play or finding a director you like and convincing them that they want to direct for little or no fee.

There are some directors who believe that writers should never direct their own work because they have a particular and personal vision of the play and might miss something that is there, waiting to be drawn out. An outside eye from an experienced director will find new things about your play you didn't even know were there. Directing calls on very particular skills which you may not have. People management and organisation abilities are the smallest of these.

Alternatively, you as the writer, certainly do have insight into your own work and can see subtleties that might otherwise be missed. It is a difficult call.

The other thing to bear in mind is that some plays will need different levels of direction.

If you take the task on yourself, not just the direction but maybe the production too, it is a lot of very time-consuming work and you have to have a budget to put in, up front. Be prepared. Even on a shoestring budget there are hidden costs. There are a number of areas that you will need to consider taking on to make your production a success.

- Hire of venue – If it is a room in a pub this can be fairly economical, often free. Sometimes, you will be asked to provide a deposit to cover staff wages if they are running an upstairs bar, for example. This is by far the most economical way of putting on a play – but by its nature, it means minimal sets, minimal casts and limited lighting.

- Hire of a theatre space – This will be more expensive. You will have to provide a deposit – usually a minimum of £50 – and enter into a contracted agreement with the theatre. This will involve some kind of split on the profits from ticket sales, with a guarantee that you will cover a minimum cost for a certain number of seats sold. For example, at least 40 seats must be sold to break even, you will have to guarantee that you will pay this or make up the difference if the audience is small.

The benefits of using a theatre space are that you will have access to lighting and a lighting technician, which you will have to pay for – and front of house, ticketing services and interval refreshments. Normally, you will be allowed into the theatre during the day before the evening's performance – and will have to get out on the same night.

If you sell all your tickets on a small studio theatre you may break even on your costs but on one night it is unlikely you will make enough to pay your cast or director. However, it can be worth doing, especially if you get reviewed and start to get your name out into the world.

There is nothing quite like the first night of a play when it has gone well. It is very special.

> 'There is nothing quite like the first night of a play when it has gone well. It is very special.'

- Budgets and hidden costs – Create a budget and be aware that there are always hidden costs. Rehearsal space needs to be found, rehearsal schedules, transport costs, props and costumes, make-up and sound. Most of all there is marketing which you will have to do yourself. The theatre will put you on their website but that's it, everything from poster/flyer design to digital media will have to be done by you or a volunteer. Get yourself interviewed on local media, get into all the listings, magazines and newspapers, send out a media release and ring people up and ask them to come and review your play. You need to make a splash and get known. Although writers write for a reason – if, like me, you don't like networking, you have to get over it and present your work to the world and let people know that it is happening.

Do not underestimate the costs involved in this area of production. Ads cost money, flyers need to be printed.

Don't forget either, when you are asking people to do things for the experience without being paid that you will still have to buy a crate of wine and give flowers and gifts. It all costs money.

- Guest lists are very useful. Get to know who the local creative arts agencies are and invite their theatre development people. They can only choose not to come, but at least you have invited them. Arts agencies want to know what is going on but it can be hard to get them along. Be direct and business-like in your dealings with them.

Living with success and failure

If there is a single personal quality that you will need as a playwright, it is stubborn determination. It is hard to write plays, hard to get them performed, hard to get noticed. Once performed, all those months of work are over in an hour or two over a few nights and all that seems to remain are a handful of photographs, maybe a review or two, and a subjective, subliminal memory in your audience's collective head.

But it is the best of arts, it is a magical, collaborative effort and it produces the kind of creative energy that doesn't exist anywhere else. Your audience is part of the process, part of the final experience of creating something amazing that touches people out of a tissue of words.

However many obstacles you face in getting your work on the stage and recognition, don't give up, it is the noblest of writing arts.

'However many obstacles you face in getting your work on the stage and recognition don't give up, it is the noblest of writing arts.'

Remind yourself of this if you get a bad or mediocre review. Often, the person reviewing, especially at a fringe level, has little experience. Look to your audience and the way they leave the theatre or the room, look at the energy that your words have generated and that will tell you a great deal.

At the same time you will need to develop a theatre skin and your own critical faculties. You will know yourself when something isn't working. This self-knowledge of what is going on with your own work is vital and will help you to accept criticism when it has purpose and is justified, and ignore anything said which has no roots in the reality of your play.

Above all keep going.

The thing about playwriting . . .

. . . is that you never stop learning and developing at whatever stage of your writing career. The life of a writer can be lonely, for a start, it is something you end up doing in odd hours when you have to earn a living too. It can be a real support to be in contact with others who have the same passion for scriptwriting that you do.

Workshops

There are always workshops on offer and they can be of varying quality and price. Teaching is very often a way of bringing in some income as a writer and you will find there are workshops offered by individual writers in the community, theatre companies will often offer workshop opportunities as part of festivals or development schemes, some of which you will have to compete for. There are writing schemes, such as at The Royal Court. There are writer development centres around the country such as The Norwich Writers' Centre which has an annual slate of workshops with professional writers at the top of their game. It is up to you if you can afford the fees. Some of them will give invaluable insight and advice and you might make friends.

Writing groups

If you are lucky there may be a writers' group near you, a like-minded group of scriptwriters who meet occasionally to share their work, read and give feedback. This can be very supportive, and if it is a good group then it will give you the kind of feedback you need. If there is not a group nearby think about starting one up.

Script readers attached to theatre companies

Remember that all script readers are very human individuals who will have very little time and far too much to read and will have their own personal preferences. Most of the time, if they are attached to a theatre company, they will be the first pair of eyes and what they will be looking for is a spark – only when they have found a spark will they maybe pass your script up the line to someone who may have the power to make something happen.

Script reading services

There are script reading services for which you can pay to have your script read and receive a written report. You can find these on the Web or if you contact any literature development agency they will point you in the right direction. The most well known is The Literacy Consultancy. They can be very helpful and offer you good advice but take a long time to reply, even with a fee. See the help list.

Summing Up

- Getting your work out there as a playwright is difficult, though there are several avenues you can explore.

- Entering your script to new writing competitions is a good way to get your work noticed.

- Approach new writing theatres and small touring companies, though be sure to contact companies that put on plays of your genre.

- Stage your play yourself. Be prepared to commit your time, effort – and money.

- To help cope with failure and bad reviews, remember to never give up.

- Pay attention to your audience's reaction, not the reviewer's.

- Attending workshops and writers' groups is a great way of finding support and inspiration, and making new friends.

Chapter Ten

Genres

There is a huge list of different genres in theatre. Here is a list of the most important.

Tragedy

A play where the main character suffers a profound downfall usually in part through the consequence of a flaw in their personality – the Greeks were the early masters of the form, their tragedies unlike Shakespeare's were entirely devoid of humour and the stakes were very high. These early plays dealt with the tragic lives of high figures, gods, kings and queens, noble families. Nowadays, tragedy is an infusion in dramatic plays – and the tragic is more likely to be understated, in the everyday grief and misery of ordinary lives.

Comedy

Comedy resembles tragedy in that the downfall of the main character is also due to a character flaw but in comedy the stakes are low.

There is a whole range of comedy forms in theatre:

- Black comedy is full of disillusion or cynicism with characters often in an absurd situation or up against incomprehensible powers. Its roots go back to the tragicomedies of Shakespeare.

- Comedy of manners has at its heart the behaviour and deportation of a group of men and women usually from the middle and upper classes.

- Comedy of morals is satirical and designed to ridicule vices like hypocrisy, pride and social pretensions.

- Comedy of intrigue depends on an intricate plot full of surprises.

- Comedy of ideas is applied to plays that debate in a witty way ideas and theories. George Bernard Shaw wrote plays in this genre.

- Farce, which is derived from the latin farcere, 'to stuff' – is designed to provide humour of the simplest kind. It is associated with burlesque by its buffoonery and low comedy. Hence plays such as *No Sex Please, We're British*. In farce, character and dialogue are nearly always subservient to plot and situation.

- Romantic comedy has love as its main theme and ends happily.

- Satirical comedy has as its purpose to expose, censure or ridicule the vices, follies and shortcomings of society.

- Musical comedy – a humorous story with humorous song and dance.

Melodrama

The origins of melodrama lie in Italy in the late 16th century and grew out of opera. It is characterised by sensationalism and extravagant emotions. Characters tend to be very black and white – exceptionally pure or villainous. Melodrama is used in comedy and thrillers and is often parodied.

Historical/chronicle drama

Plays in this genre are based on recorded history rather than myths or legends. Most notable modern historical plays include Arthur Miller's *The Crucible* and Robert Bolt's *A Man for all Seasons.*

Thrillers

Exciting, tautly plotted theatre of suspense where a mystery needs to be resolved.

Musical theatre

The emphasis is on the music but a strong story is also needed. *The Threepenny Opera* by Kurt Weill and Bertolt Brecht, or *The Phantom of the Opera* by Andrew Lloyd Webber are examples.

Pantomime

Its roots lie in Harlequin, but pantomime is a very specific form of musical theatre, a spectacular Christmas entertainment aimed at children. It has very specific requirements such as a principal boy (the hero played by a female actor), the pantomime dame, played by a male actor, and plenty of slapstick.

Theatre of the absurd

At the heart of this genre is the idea that Man is absurd and much of his behaviour. This theatre grew out of a group of dramatists, principle among them, Samuel Beckett. The plays lack conventional structure and formal logic.

Theatre of the absurd has influenced much modern writing.

Epic theatre

This form of theatre originated in Berlin in the 1920s – and was theatre designed to appeal to reason rather than emotion. It was also known as alienation theatre. Bertolt Brecht was its main exponent. It generally has a linear narration and is didactic. It uses a chorus, addresses the audience directly and comments on the play and is often used to express political ideas.

Kitchen sink drama

A powerful form of writing developed in the 1950s to 1960s in Britain – focusing on working-class lives. Major writers include John Osborne and Arnold Wesker.

Monologues (one woman/man shows)

This is a genre where one performer address the audience. Monologues are often a constituent of other plays.

Physical theatre

As it sounds, uses physical movement and expression to convey story.

A final word

It feels too abrupt to just leave you with a list of possible things to do with your finished play. The thing is, I hope that your first play will lead to writing many others until you have a body of work.

Whatever you do with your work, I hope that you will have a passion for writing that will stay with you and be a joyous adventure that goes on for as long as you can lift a pen.

I came to scriptwriting almost entirely by accident, but I am so glad that I did. It has a kind of power to energise that no other form of writing offers. It is 3D writing and lifts off the page.

Write every day and celebrate your efforts. You are one of that tribe of ardent scribblers who puts words together and changes the world a little.

Help List

Arts Council

www.artscouncil.org.uk/

Sign up for Arts News and daily emails in your inbox of job/commission opportunities. Follow developments in arts policy and funding and research

and apply for funding where applicable.

BBC Writer's Room

www.bbc.co.uk/writersroom

This is an invaluable website because it is full of helpful tips, scripts to read and opportunities for competitions. It covers scriptwriting for radio, film and TV, but posts playwriting opportunities on its website. Great blog!

Mslexia

www.mslexia.co.uk

Quarterly magazine for women who write and runs workshops and courses, provides helpful advice.

The Writers' Guild of Great Britain

www.writersguild.org.uk

The Writer's Guild supports writers and scriptwriters with lots of helpful advice about rates of pay, contracts and awards. It is a campaigning organisation among other things. Membership isn't cheap but it is definitely worth visiting their website. It has a great weekly blog delivered straight to your inbox which will keep you up to date with the industry.

WritersMarket.com

www.writersmarket.com

Provides market information – US-based – but there is a script market online. General industry information.

Development

The Arvon Foundation
www.arvonfoundation.org/
Courses taught by professional writers in beautiful surroundings.

The Drama Association of Wales
www.dramawales.org.uk
Script reading service and playwright support.

International Theatre Council
www.itc-arts.org
Provides a range of services for performing arts companies.

The Literacy Consultancy
www.literaryconsultancy.co.uk
Professional mentoring schemes, writing holiday adventures, script reading service.

National Association for Literature Development
www.literaturedevelopment.co.uk/
Professional development site with job and commission opportunities.

New Writing North
www.newwritingnorth.com/
New writing development agency for the North East.

Playwright's Studio Scotland
www.playwrightsstudio.co.uk
Writing development agency for Scotland.

Pier Playwrights (New Writing South)

www.newwritingsouth.com/

Pier Playwrights run Chichester Young Playwrights development scheme among other programmes to support new writers. They also provide a mentoring service, script reading and all manner of support.

The Script Factory

www.scriptfactory.co.uk

West Midlands regional development agency.

Script Online

www.scriptonline.net

West Midlands regional development agency.

Script Yorkshire

www.scriptyorkshire.org.uk

Writing development agency for Yorkshire.

Sherman Cymru

www.shermancymru.co.uk

Welsh playwriting development agency.

South West Scriptwriter

www.southwest-scriptwriters.co.uk

Supportive scriptwriters' writing development agency.

Theatre Writing Partnership

www.theatrewritingpartnership.org.uk/

East Midlands writer development agency.

Write On – Cambridge scriptwriting forum

www.writeon.org.uk/

Prizes and Competitions

The Alfred Fagon Award

www.alfredfagonaward.co.uk
An annual award of £5,000 for the best new play written by someone of Caribbean descent.

The Bruntwood Prize for Playwriting

www.writeaplay.co.uk/about
A biennial competition with £16,000 award for the winning play and production.

International Playwriting Festival

www.warehousetheatre.co.uk
An annual international playwriting festival for full-length and unperformed plays – selected entries are performed during the festival.

The Windsor Fringe Kenneth Branagh Award for New Writing

www.windsorfringe.co.uk
One-act, 30-minute plays for amateur playwrights with production and a cash prize for the winner.

Verity Bargate Award

Soho Theatre and Writers' Centre
www.sohotheatre.com/
The foremost new writing/playwriting award in the UK – it is a biennial competition open to an unperformed full-length play. The prize is £5,000 and a residency at the Soho Theatre plus production.

New writing theatres

The Bush Theatre

www.bushtheatre.co.uk
Promotes, produces and develops new writing – reading about 1,500 scripts a year. Dedicated to getting back to the writer of a new play in 8 weeks.

Hull Truck Theatre Company

www.hulltruck.co.uk/

Provides free reading service, short play commissions and a festival.

The Liverpool Everyman and Playhouse Theatre

www.everymanplayhouse.com

Offers substantial support, new writing festival and young writers' festival.

Menagerie

www.menagerietheatre.co.uk

The leading new writing theatre company in the East of England – it holds an annual new writing festival – Hotbed.

Octagon Theatre, Bolton

www.octagonbolton.co.uk

Script development, playwright attachments and a script reading service.

Polka Theatre

www.polkatheatre.com

A world class theatre with support for new writing for children and young people.

The Royal Court Theatre

www.royalcourttheatre.com/

The Royal Court's literary department reads 3000 unsolicited scripts from new and emerging writers a year and is deeply committed to finding exciting new work. It also hosts an annual new young playwriting festival.

Soho Theatre

www.sohotheatre.com

The Soho Theatre has been the investing new writing theatre for over 25 years. It offers a series of workshops and courses as well as writer development schemes, including The Hub which provides opportunities for new writers to see their work produced.

Theatre Royal Stratford East

www.stratfordeast.com
Accepts unsolicited scripts but will not return scripts and will only be in touch if they wish to work with you.

Glossary

Allegory
A symbolic narrative. Allegory often takes the form of a story in which the characters represent moral qualities.

Alliteration
The repetition of consonant sounds, especially at the beginning of words. Example: 'Wild winds whistle through these word woods.'

Antagonist
A character or force against which another character struggles.

Aside
Words spoken by an actor directly to the audience, which are not heard by the other characters on stage during a play.

Assonance
The repetition of similar vowel sounds in a sentence or a line of poetry or prose.

Catastrophe
The action at the end of a tragedy that initiates the falling action of a play.

Catharsis
The purging of the feelings of pity and fear that, according to Aristotle, occur in the audience of tragic drama. The audience experiences catharsis at the end of the play, following the catastrophe.

Character
An imaginary person that inhabits a literary work. Literary characters may be major or minor, static (unchanging) or dynamic (capable of change).

Characterization
The way character is revealed; although techniques of characterization are complex, writers typically reveal characters through their speech, dress, manner, and actions.

Chorus

A group of characters in Greek tragedy (and in later forms of drama), who comment on the action of a play without participation in it. Their leader is the choragos. Sophocles' *Antigone* and *Oedipus the King* both contain an explicit chorus with a choragos.

Climax

The turning point of the action in the plot of a play or story. The climax represents the point of greatest tension in the work.

Comedy

A type of drama in which the characters experience reversals of fortune, usually for the better. In comedy, things work out happily in the end. Comic drama may be either romantic – characterised by a tone of tolerance and geniality – or satiric. Satiric works offer a darker vision of human nature, one that ridicules human folly.

Comic relief

The use of a comic scene to interrupt a succession of intensely tragic dramatic moments. The comedy of scenes offering comic relief typically parallels the tragic action that the scenes interrupt. Comic relief is lacking in Greek tragedy, but occurs regularly in Shakespeare's tragedies.

Complication

An intensification of the conflict in a story or play. Complication builds up, accumulates, and develops the primary or central conflict in a literary work.

Conflict

A struggle between opposing forces in a story or play, usually resolved by the end of the work. The conflict may occur within a character as well as between characters.

Connotation

The associations called up by a word that goes beyond its dictionary meaning.

Convention

A customary feature of a literary work, such as the use of a chorus in Greek tragedy, the inclusion of an explicit moral in a fable, or the use of a particular rhyme scheme in a villanelle. Literary conventions are defining features of particular literary genres, such as novel, short story, ballad, sonnet, and play.

Denotation

The dictionary meaning of a word. Writers typically play off a word's denotative meaning against its connotations, or suggested and implied associational implications.

Denouement

The resolution of the plot of a literary work. The denouement of Hamlet takes place after the catastrophe, with the stage littered with corpses.

Deus ex machine

A god who resolves the entanglements of a play by supernatural intervention. The Latin phrase means, literally 'a god from the machine' The phrase refers to the use of artificial means to resolve the plot of a play.

Dialogue

The conversation of characters in a literary work. In fiction, dialogue is typically enclosed within quotation marks. In plays, characters' speech is preceded by their names.

Diction

The selection of words in a literary work. A work's diction forms one of its centrally important literary elements, as writers use words to convey action, reveal character, imply attitudes, identify themes and suggest values.

Dramatic monologue

A type of poem in which an imaginary speaker addresses an imaginary listener. As readers, we overhear the speaker in a dramatic monologue.

Dramatis personae

Latin for the characters or persons in a play.

Exposition

The first stage of a fictional or dramatic plot, in which necessary background information is provided.

Fable

A brief story with an explicit moral provided by the author. Fables typically include animals as characters.

Metonymy
A figure of speech in which a closely related term is substituted for an object or idea.

Monologue
A speech by a single character without another character's response.

Narrator
The voice and implied speaker of a fictional work, to be distinguished from the actual living author.

Onomatopoeia
The use of words to imitate the sounds they describe. Words such as 'buzz' and 'crack' are onomatopoeic.

Parody
A humorous, mocking imitation of a literary work, but often playful and even respectful in its playful imitation.

Pathos
A quality of a play's action that stimulates the audience to feel pity for a character. Pathos is always an aspect of tragedy, and may be present in comedy as well.

Personification
The endowment of inanimate objects or abstract concepts with animate or living qualities.

Plot
The unified structure of incidents in a play or work of fiction.

Point of view
The angle of vision from which a story is narrated. See Narrator. A work's point of view can be: first person, in which the narrator is a character or an observer, respectively; objective, in which the narrator knows or appears to know no more than the reader; omniscient, in which the narrator knows everything about the characters; and limited omniscient, which allows the narrator to know some things about the characters but not everything.

Props
Articles or objects that appear on stage during a play.

Protagonist
The main character in a script or story.

Recognition
The point at which a character understands his or her situation as it really is. Othello comes to an understanding of his situation in Act V of *Othello*.

Resolution
The sorting out or unravelling of a plot at the end of a play, novel, or story.

Reversal
The point at which the action of the plot turns in an unexpected direction for the protagonist. Othello's recognition is a reversal. They learn what they did not expect to learn.

Rising action
A set of conflicts and crises that constitute the part of a play's or story's plot leading up to the climax.

Satire
A literary work that criticises human misconduct and ridicules vices, stupidities, and follies.

Setting
The time and place of a drama that establishes context.

Soliloquy
A speech in a play that is meant to be heard by the audience but not by other characters on the stage. If there are no other characters present, the soliloquy represents the character thinking aloud.

Stage direction
A playwright's descriptive or interpretive comments that provide readers (and actors) with information about the dialogue, setting and action of a play.

Staging
The spectacle a play presents in performance, including the position of actors on stage, the scenic background, the props and costumes, and the lighting and sound effects. Tennessee Williams describes these in his detailed stage directions for *The Glass Menagerie* and also in his production notes for the play.

Style
The way an author chooses words, arranges them in sentences or in lines of dialogue or verse, and develops ideas and actions with description, imagery, and other literary techniques.

Subject
What a story or play is about; to be distinguished from plot and theme.

Subplot
A subsidiary or subordinate or parallel plot in a play or story that coexists with the main plot. The story of Rosencrantz and Guildenstern forms a subplot with the overall plot of *Hamlet*.

Subtext
The under or below text of what is not said or not done. It denotes the unspoken in a play. It can also apply to the 'shape' of a plot or the pattern of imagery within the play.

Symbol
An object or action in a literary work that means more than itself, that stands for something beyond itself.

Synecdoche
A figure of speech in which a part is substituted for the whole.

Theme
The idea of a literary work abstracted from its details of language, character, and action, and cast in the form of a generalisation.

Tone
The implied attitude of a writer toward the subject and characters of a work.

Tragedy
A type of drama in which the characters experience reversals of fortune, usually for the worse. In tragedy, catastrophe and suffering await many of the characters, especially the protagonist.

Tragic flaw
A weakness or limitation of character, resulting in the fall of the tragic hero. Othello's jealousy is an example.

Need2Know

Tragic hero

A privileged, exalted character of high repute, who, by virtue of a tragic flaw and fate, suffers a fall from glory into suffering, for example, Hamlet.

Understatement

A figure of speech in which a writer or speaker says less than what he or she means; the opposite of exaggeration.

Unities

The idea that a play should be limited to a specific time, place and storyline. The events of the plot should occur within a twenty-four hour period, should occur within a specific location, and should tell a single story.

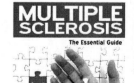